THEORY OF PORTFOLIO SELECTION

STUDIES IN FINANCE AND ACCOUNTING

General Editors: M. J. Barron and D. W. Pearce

Published

Michael Firth: MANAGEMENT OF WORKING CAPITAL

Michael Firth: THE VALUATION OF SHARES AND THE EFFICIENT-MARKETS THEORY

Kenneth Midgley and Ronald Burns: THE CAPITAL MARKET: ITS NATURE AND SIGNIFICANCE

Terence M. Ryan: THEORY OF PORTFOLIO SELECTION

Robert W. Scapens: ACCOUNTING IN AN INFLATIONARY ENVIRONMENT

Forthcoming

M. J. Barron: BUSINESS FINANCE THEORY

M. J. Barron: MATRIX MODELS FOR ACCOUNTING

Brian Quinn: MULTINATIONAL BUSINESS FINANCE AND ACCOUNTING

Charles Sutcliffe: ECONOMICS VERSUS ACCOUNTANCY

Theory of Portfolio Selection

TERENCE M. RYAN, M.A.

Trinity College, University of Dublin

First published 1978 by
THE MACMILLAN PRESS LTD
London and Basingstoke
Associated companies in Delhi Dublin
Hong Kong Johannesburg Lagos Melbourne
New York Singapore and Tokyo

Typeset in Great Britain by
REDWOOD BURN LIMITED
Trowbridge & Esher
Printed and bound in Hong Kong

British Library Cataloguing in Publication Data

Ryan, Terence M
  Theory of portfolio selection – (Studies in
  finance and accounting).
  1. Investments
  I. Title II. Series
  332.6′7   HG4539

  ISBN 0–333–23306–9
  ISBN 0–333–17686–3 Pbk

Contents

General Editors' Preface

The last few years have been very exciting for research in finance and accounting. An enormous amount has happened, and in many cases traditional thinking and traditional solutions have been completely overthrown. At the same time it is quite clear that research into the theory and, perhaps even more important, into British empirical evidence, will continue to accumulate rapidly. While this is fine for the researcher in his detailed specialist world, it is not so good for the student who wants to acquire a relatively straightforward but up-to-date overview of the subject.

The 'Macmillan Studies in Finance and Accounting' set out to provide short, reasonably critical surveys of the developments within the various specialist areas of business finance and accounting. The emphasis in each study is upon recent work, but each topic will generally be placed in a historical context so that the reader may see the logical development of thought through time. Selected bibliographies are provided to guide readers to more extensive works. Each study aims at a brief treatment of the salient problems in order to avoid clouding the issues in too much detailed argument.

Unfortunately it is inevitable that in a few areas the level of mathematics will be rather near the limit for some students. This is because the rigorous methods of statistics, econometrics and mathematical economics have made a considerable contribution to the research achievements in the subject. Thus, although all the authors in the series have tried hard to make their presentation as lucid as possible there is a point beyond which mathematical arguments cannot be explained non-mathematically except at a superficial level. Nevertheless intuition can go a long way and many students, even with very little mathematical background, have found that the intrinsic fascination of the subject more than compensates for occasional difficulty.

M. J. Barron
D. W. Pearce

CHAPTER 1

A Framework for Portfolio Selection

What is a Portfolio?

Most people if asked the above question would immediately think of a *portfolio* as consisting of a collection of financial or real assets such as equity shares, bonds, treasury bills, property, debentures and so on. Indeed, in defining a portfolio in such terms one would not be far wrong since the large institutional portfolios of the insurance companies, pension funds, unit trusts, building societies, banks and similar bodies which play such an important role in the financing and ownership of the country's capital do in fact consist predominantly of such assets.

However, to define a portfolio simply in terms of such assets is to unnecessarily delimit the meaning of the concept and, by implication, the applicability of portfolio-selection theory. In a more general sense the term 'portfolio' may be used synonymously with the expression 'collection of assets'. The collector of old Persian rugs, of coins, of silver, of old masters is in each case selecting a portfolio. Can the theory of portfolio selection expounded in this book provide any guidelines for the manner in which such collections or portfolios should be constructed?

In order to answer this important question it is first necessary to distinguish between portfolios which are held purely for *consumption* purposes and those which are held purely for *investment* purposes. If a wine collector lays down a cellar of classic wines he may, in our terminology, be said to have a portfolio of wines. In order to ascertain whether the theory of portfolio selection can offer any guidance to him on the best way of constructing this portfolio, it would be necessary to know whether his purpose in laying down the wines was simply to enjoy consuming them at a later date, or whether he intended to sell them later on with a view to making a profit. In the former case the theory of portfolio selection has no advice to offer to our wine-lover – he will simply purchase those wines which offer him the maximum anticipated enjoyment. In the latter case, however, the theory developed in this book will have quite a lot to say about the optimal composition of the wine cellar.

Another area where the theory of portfolio selection has been widely applied with considerable success is agriculture. The typical farmer in choosing his livestock and crop mix is making a portfolio–selection decision no less complicated or important than that made by the investment manager of a large London insurance company. The formal structures of both problems are exactly the same, as are the principles which determine the optimal solutions.

In short, then, whenever there is a problem of choosing a mix of assets for investment purposes, be they financial or real (i.e. physical), or both, then there exists a situation in which the principles that constitute the theory of portfolio selection should properly be applied.

Any given portfolio may well include liabilities as well as assets. However, from the point of view of the theory of portfolio selection, a liability may be treated simply as if it were an asset with a negative return. Consequently, while the discussion in this book refers primarily to the theory of asset selection, the same theoretical structure may be applied with equal legitimacy to the problem of liability selection – and indeed to the simultaneous selection of both assets and liabilities.[1]

The Five Stages of Portfolio Management

The expression 'portfolio management' is a collective term for a wide range of activities. These activities may broadly speaking be classified under the following five headings: (i) the definition of the portfolio's objective and the constraints under which it is held; (ii) the choice of an asset universe, or opportunity set, from which the portfolio is to be drawn; (iii) formulation of the decision rules, or criteria, on which to build the portfolio; (iv) the estimation of the relevant characteristics of the individual assets in the asset universe, and, on the basis of such evaluation, their inclusion in, or omission from, the portfolio; and (v) establishing the criteria for monitoring the performance of the portfolio through time and for changing its composition whenever and wherever it is deemed necessary.

The first step in constructing a portfolio is to set out explicitly the objective that one is pursuing, and also the nature of any constraints, legal or institutional, which might delimit the range of assets eligible for inclusion in the portfolio, or the amount of any single asset that may be held.

The objective to be pursued will invariably be stated in terms of the investor's utility function, and in Chapter 2 we explore the theoretical foundations of utility theory, particularly as it is applied to the problem of portfolio selection.

The constraints may be of several types. In certain circumstances, for example, all assets in the portfolio may be required to be of trustee status, or there may be legally imposed or self-imposed liquidity requirements implying that the proportion of the fund held in the form of liquid assets should not fall below a certain figure.

It is also desirable to know at the outset the length of time for which the portfolio is to be held – the holding horizon – and the length of time that will elapse between revisions or reviews of the composition of the portfolio – the review horizon. In the literature on portfolio management, time is divided up into periods of equal length, each period being the same length as the review horizon. Decisions concerning the composition of the portfolio may only be undertaken at the beginning of such a time period, and any decision taken then is binding until the end of that period, when it may be changed. It is usually necessary to know whether the investor intends to liquidate his portfolio at the end of the next period and consume his wealth, or intends to continue holding a portfolio. As we shall see in Chapter 8 the optimal composition of his portfolio will in general vary with the answer to the above.

STAGE TWO

The identification of the universe of assets from which it is proposed to construct the portfolio is an important though often neglected stage in the task of portfolio selection. The total number of assets in existence is virtually infinite. Consequently, if one is to make an informed choice among these various assets, one must of necessity confine one's attention to a sub-set of all the assets which are actually available. This sub-set is then regarded as the relevant asset universe, and any assets not in this universe are simply ignored from the point of view of portfolio selection. Very often the defining of the asset universe presents no particular problem, in that many institutional portfolios are restricted to clearly defined asset groups, such as property portfolios, commodity portfolios, and so on. However, the problem is not always so simple. There are, unfortunately, no hard-and-fast rules for deciding either on the size or the composition of the asset universe. Too large an asset universe will involve the investor in needless costs, since the cost of acquiring and processing information is roughly proportional to the size of the universe. In Chapter 6 we explore the underlying principles which will at least provide some guidelines for deciding on an appropriate asset universe.

STAGE THREE

For the investor, having decided upon his objective and on the instruments (the assets) for attaining it, the next stage in the portfolio-selection process is the formulation of a set of decision rules which, on the basis of information to be gathered in stage four, enable the investor to select, from among those assets which constitute the universe, the ones which best contribute to the attainment of his objective. The principles on which such decision rules are based form the subject-matter of Chapter 5.

It is only in the light of such decision rules that one can decide on what it is that constitutes the relevant characteristics of the individual assets in the universe. Different decision rules will lead to a different set of relevant characteristics.

The application of the decision rule(s) will determine which assets are to be included in the portfolio, and in what quantities. Typically the assets chosen for inclusion will be just a small proportion of the total asset universe. Those assets which are not included in the port-folio do not, however, become irrelevant, nor should the information on them be discarded. They form the appropriate pool from which any subsequent alterations in the composition of the portfolio should be made. A portfolio rarely remains optimal indefinitely, even though optimal when first selected. In fact the major recurring task of port-folio management is the continual updating of the composition of the portfolio, and this activity takes place within the confines imposed by the chosen asset universe.

STAGE FOUR

In order to make the decision rules developed in stage three operational, it is next necessary to assemble information on the relevant technological, economic and statistical characteristics of each asset in the asset universe and to condense this information in such a way as to enable the investor to apply the decision rules. This activity, which is highly specialised and calls for a considerable degree of skill and judgement, is the domain of the financial analyst.[2]

Although the volume of data on each asset required for the successful implementation of portfolio-selection theory (especially in index form) can be relatively small, the major contribution of the security analyst is in ensuring a high degree of quality or reliability in these statistical inputs.

STAGE FIVE

Although the initial portfolio has been selected at stage four, the task of portfolio management has just begun. The commercial and financial world is in a continuous state of change: stocks which once performed well may lose their appeal, or new desirable stocks may come into existence. The practice of portfolio management involves a continual response to such changes – by altering the composition of the portfolio when and where appropriate. The principles governing the optimal revision of the portfolio are described in Chapter 8.

Portfolio revision is as much an art as it is a science, in that it entails a considerable degree of judgement and interpretation of new information. A person who responds too eagerly to every new item of information will incur unnecessary brokerage costs by constantly changing the composition of his portfolio. Such costs can quite easily eat up most or all of the profit which an undisturbed portfolio could generate.

On the other hand, an investor who fails to respond to market signals, and who continues to regard his initial portfolio as optimal in the face of changing circumstances, runs a high risk of being left behind by events and of making a lower rate of return on his wealth than he might have done by a more diligent review of his portfolio. Unfortunately, the ability to steer a safe course between these two rocks is something which can only be gained by experience and cannot be learnt from a textbook.

CHAPTER 2

Utility Theory and Decision-making under Uncertainty

The outcome of virtually every decision that we take is affected to a greater or lesser extent by the existence of *uncertainty*. For example, the decision about where to spend one's vacation will most likely be influenced by uncertainty about the amount of sunshine one expects, the standard of the hotel, the possibility of the tour operator going bankrupt, the likelihood of arriving safely, and so on.

Yet despite the great number of imponderables in even as straightforward a decision as the above, we all continue to make such decisions regularly without too much fuss and bother, so that coping with uncertainty has become so much a part of our nature that we are scarcely aware that we are doing it.

We are concerned in this book with the analysis of a particular type of decision-making problem – namely the decision as to how to divide one's wealth between the various types of assets that are available. It is scarcely necessary to make the point that the existence of uncertainty concerning the future value of individual assets must play a predominant role in influencing one's behaviour in this sphere.

This portfolio-selection problem is, in a formal sense, nothing more than a specific example of the general problem of decision-making under uncertainty. The latter is an area in which a considerable body of theory has evolved, and so in order to develop a theory capable of resolving the portfolio-selection problem we shall find it fruitful to look first at the general theory of decision-making under uncertainty.

The fundamental concept which underpins the whole theory of decision-making under uncertainty is that of *utility* – a concept which has for many years played a prominent role in the fields of economics and psychology.

Utility Theory

Initially the utility concept implied the ability to measure happiness, or satisfaction – the units of measurement being called 'utils'. In this form the utility concept underpinned choice theory until the 1930s when it was gradually superseded by the Hicksian indifference-curve analysis[1] which dispensed with the notion that happiness or satisfaction could be measured – an assumption which was becoming an increasing embarrassment to economists in view of their conspicuous failure to measure it.

Utility theory re-emerged under a new guise in the post-war years as a result of the path-breaking work of von Neumann and Morgenstern.[2] However, the modern concept of utility has little in common with the earlier version, having stemmed from work on the theory of rational decision-making under conditions of uncertainty.

The concept of *rationality* plays a very important role in modern utility theory, and our first task is to define carefully what we mean by the term 'rational behaviour'.

RATIONAL BEHAVIOUR

The axioms which define rational behaviour are best expressed in terms of *binary relationships*. A binary relationship is simply a relationship which holds between two objects. Thus, for example, if John (whom we shall denote by the letter j) is taller than David (whom we shall denote by d), then we may formally express the above binary relationship by

$$j \; T \; d,$$

where T is simply a symbol to denote the binary relationship 'is taller than'.

The binary relationships which form the building blocks for the concept of rational behaviour correspond to the common-sense notion of 'preference'. They are three in number:

(1) the *strong-preference* relationship, written $A \succ B$, which asserts that A is strictly preferred to B, where A and B are two events, or states of the world;

(2) the *indifference* relationship, written $A \sim B$, which asserts that the individual is indifferent as between the occurrence of A or B (i.e. neither one is preferred to the other);

(3) the *weak-preference* relationship, written $A \succcurlyeq B$, which asserts

that A is either preferred to B or is indifferent to B, or, to put it another way, B is *not* strictly preferred to A.

Using the above three binary relationships, rational behaviour may now be defined as behaviour which conforms to the following five axioms.

Axiom 1: Comparability

Every pair of events (we shall denote a typical pair by e_i and e_j) must be comparable by the weak-preference relationship, i.e. the decision-maker must be able to say either that

$$e_i \succcurlyeq e_j,$$

or that

$$e_j \succcurlyeq e_i.$$

He may of course assert the truth of both statements, which would imply

$$e_i \sim e_j.$$

The necessity for this axiom is fairly obvious – in that an individual who cannot even make a comparison between two events or objects is scarcely in a position to make a rational choice between them.

Axiom 2: Transitivity

For every triad of possible events (e.g. e_i, e_j and e_k) if $e_i \succcurlyeq e_j$ and $e_j \succcurlyeq e_k$ then transitivity implies that

$$e_i \succcurlyeq e_k.$$

Similarly, if $e_i \sim e_j$ and $e_j \sim e_k$ then transitivity implies that

$$e_i \sim e_k.$$

The concept of 'transitivity' thus corresponds to the common-sense notion of consistency in a person's preferences. An individual who prefers cigars to cigarettes, snuff to cigars, and cigarettes to snuff, will, to say the least, have difficulty in making a rational choice between the three.

Axiom 3: Strong Independence

In order to state this axiom we need to introduce some new notation. By the expression

$$G(e_i, e_k | p)$$

we denote a lottery or gamble which will result either in the outcome e_i with probability of occurrence p, or the outcome e_k with probability $1-p$. The strong independence axiom states that the binary relation which holds between any two events is not affected when they are each combined in a lottery with an arbitrary third event. Thus:

$$\text{if} \quad e_i \succcurlyeq e_j, \text{ then } G(e_i, e_k | p) \succcurlyeq G(e_j, e_k | p);$$
$$\text{or if} \quad e_i \sim e_j, \text{ then } G(e_i, e_k | p) \sim G(e_j, e_k | p);$$
$$\text{lastly, if } e_i \succ e_j, \text{ then } G(e_i, e_k | p) \succ G(e_j, e_k | p).$$

The axiom requires the above conditions to hold for *every* pair of possible events when combined with *any* third event at *any* level of probability. This axiom is sometimes referred to as the axiom of *the independence of irrelevant alternatives.*

Axiom 4: Existence of an Indifferent Gamble

If the event e_i is strictly preferred to the event e_k,

$$e_i \succ e_k,$$

and if the level of preference for the event e_j lies somewhere between the two

$$\left\{ \begin{array}{l} e_i \succcurlyeq e_j \\ e_j \succcurlyeq e_k \end{array} \right.$$

then there exists a unique level of probability, denoted by p_j, such that

$$e_j \sim G(e_i, e_k | p_j),$$

which states that the investor will be indifferent as between the occurrence of the event e_j and the gamble that either e_i or e_k will result (p_j being the probability that e_i will be the outcome).

In addition, consider any other event, say e_l, the level of preference for which also lies between that of e_i and e_k, i.e.

$$e_i \succcurlyeq e_l$$
$$e_l \succcurlyeq e_k$$

then, from the above, there exists a unique level of probability p_l such that

$$e_l \sim G(e_i, e_k | p_l).$$

In addition $p_i > p_j$ implies that $e_i \succ e_j$ and $p_i = p_j$ implies that $e_i \sim e_j$.

Axiom 5: Existence of Non-empty Choice Set

There exists a *most preferred event*, which we shall denote by e_m, such that $e_m \succeq e_i$, where e_i is any other possible event. There also exists a *least preferred event*, e_l, such that $e_i \succeq e_l$. Lastly, $e_m \succ e_l$.

This last axiom is necessary in order to eliminate from the analysis individuals who are indifferent as between all possible states of the world. Clearly for such people no problem of choice exists.

THE EXPECTED UTILITY THEOREM

Probably the most important single contribution to modern utility theory is the *expected utility theorem* as propounded by von Neumann and Morgenstern. They demonstrated that if an individual behaves rationally, in the sense that his behaviour is in accordance with the above five axioms of rationality, then it is possible to assign a number, called 'utility', to each possible event, e_i, written:

$$U = U(e_i),$$

for example, $7 =$ the utility of (receiving £10). This number has the following properties:

(i) if $e_i \succ e_j$, then $U(e_i) > U(e_j)$;
(ii) if $e_i \sim e_j$, then $U(e_i) = U(e_j)$;
(iii) the utility of a gamble is the weighted sum of the utilities of all the possible outcomes, the weights being the corresponding probabilities of occurrence – thus

$$U(G(e_i, e_j | p)) = pU(e_i) + (1 - p)U(e_j). \tag{2.1}$$

The utility of a gamble is usually referred to as its *expected utility*, since it is the expected value or mean of the utilities of the possible outcomes of the gamble.

The expected utility theorem thus asserts that *a rational individual, under conditions of uncertainty, will choose that action which maximises his expected utility.*[3] This is the fundamental principle which underpins the whole theory of decision-making under uncertainty.

At this stage a numerical example may help to clarify matters. Consider an individual whose utility-of-wealth function is as illustrated in Figure 2.1. The utility-of-wealth function is simply a function which assigns a number, called 'utility', to each possible level of wealth. This function will vary from one person to another, and indeed for a given person it will typically vary from one point in time to another.

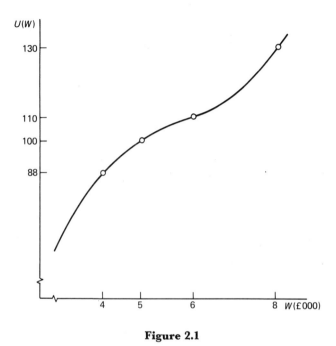

Figure 2.1

The individual whose preferences are summarised by the utility function in Figure 2.1 is offered a choice of two gambles, only one of which he may accept (he may, however, refuse both). The various possible outcomes of these gambles, together with their corresponding probabilities of occurrence, are shown in the first two columns of Table 2.1. If the individual acts rationally, which gamble will he take? Or will he refuse both?

According to the expected utility theorem he will choose that course of action which maximises the expected utility to him of the outcome. The calculations which solve the problem are very straight-forward and appear in the last three columns of Table 2.1. Column 3 lists the level of utility attached to each possible outcome, these levels being simply read off the graph in Figure 2.1.

Column 4 weights the utility of each outcome by the probability of

Table 2.1

	Possible outcomes (resulting wealth) ($£$)	Probability of occurrence	Utility of outcome	Utility weighted by probability	Expected utility
First gamble	4000	0.5	88	44	99
	6000	0.5	110	55	
Second gamble	4000	0.4	88	35.2	107.2
	6000	0.3	110	33	
	8000	0.3	130	39	
Status quo	5000	1.0	100	100	100

that outcome actually occurring. Thus, for example, in the first gamble the outcome $£$4000 will occur with a probability of 0.5. Consequently the utility measure of $£$4000, which is 88, is weighted by 0.5 to become 44.

The last column then calculates the expected utility of each option by summing up the relevant weighted utilities of outcomes. Thus the utility of the first gamble is (in the notation of the previous section):

$$U[G(£4000, £6000|0.5)] = 0.5\ U(£4000) + 0.5\ U(£6000)$$
$$= 0.5\ (88) \qquad + 0.5\ (110)$$
$$= 99.$$

The last column of Table 2.1 therefore provides us with the answer to the problem. A rational individual, having a utility-of-wealth function as described by Figure 2.1, will choose the second gamble – its expected utility (107.2) being higher than either that of the *status quo* (100) or of the first gamble (99).

RISK-AVERSION

Observe that although the first gamble is fair – in the sense that the individual has an equal chance of either gaining or losing $£$1000 – he will not accept it (even if the second gamble was not available). Such an individual who will not accept a fair gamble is said to be *risk-averse* or to be a *risk-averter*. In the above example the utility gain in winning $£$1000 is outweighed by the utility loss in losing $£$1000, and given that both events are equally likely the over-all outcome to the individual would be a reduction in the level of his expected utility. Such an individual derives successively smaller increments of utility from each additional pound of wealth which is accumulated. In other words he experiences *diminishing marginal utility of wealth*. His utility-of-wealth function will then be concave – which is to say that it increases at a diminishing rate (as in Figure 2.2(i)). A concave utility-of-wealth function is both a necessary and sufficient condition for the individual to be a risk-averter.

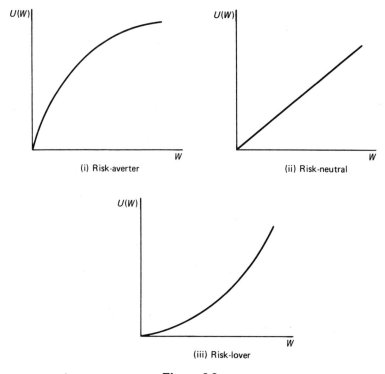

Figure 2.2

The opposite to a risk-averter is someone who will accept a gamble even if it is unfair (i.e. even if his expected money losses exceed his expected money gains). Such a person is said to be a *risk-lover*, and his utility-of-wealth function is convex (as in Figure 2.2(iii)), reflecting his increasing marginal utility of wealth.

The dividing line between risk-averters and risk-lovers is shown by someone who will just accept a gamble if it is fair, but not if it is unfair. Such individuals are said to be *risk-neutral*, and their utility-of-wealth functions are both* concave and convex – i.e. straight lines (see Figure 2.2.(ii)).

INSURANCE AND GAMBLING

An individual who does not wish to undertake risk often has the option of insuring himself against it. However, it is not at all uncommon for a person to be a confirmed gambler while at the same time holding substantial insurance policies (for example on his house or his life). Is such behaviour irrational? Not necessarily – and the reason may be seen by referring to Figure 2.3, which illustrates the utility function of an individual who is a risk-averter over some ranges of wealth and a risk-lover over others.

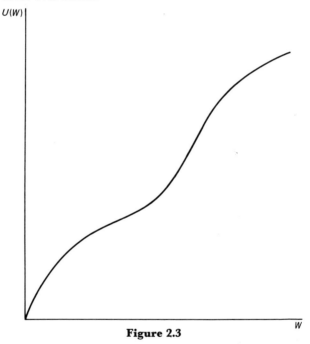

Figure 2.3

CARDINAL AND ORDINAL UTILITY

A major point of difference between the classical and modern con-

---

*Formally, the function $y = f(x)$ is said to be concave if, for any three points x_1, x_2 and x_3 such that $x_1 \leqslant x_2 \leqslant x_3$, then
$$f(x_2) \leqslant af(x_1) + (1-a)f(x_3)$$
for all values of a such that $0 \leqslant a \leqslant 1$. The function is said to be convex if the direction of the inequality sign in the displayed expression is reversed.

cepts of utility is that the former was a *cardinal* measure; that is to say, a utility level of 20 utils represented exactly twice as much satisfaction to the individual as a utility level of 10 utils. However, the modern concept of utility carries no such connotations; it is an *ordinal* measure – that is to say, a utility level of 20 units is certainly preferable to one of 10 units, but it is impossible, and indeed unnecessary, to say whether it is twice as preferable, a hundred times more preferable, or whatever. It is simply preferable.

In fact it is a simple matter to establish that von Neumann–Morgenstern-type utility functions are not unique. They are only unique up to an increasing linear transformation. This means that if $U(W)$ is a particular utility function, then $Z(W)$, which is defined as

$$Z(W) = A + BU(W), \qquad (2.2)$$

where A and B are arbitrary constants with $B > 0$, is an equally valid utility function for the same individual, in the sense that $Z(W)$ reflects his preferences in exactly the same way as does $U(W)$. Thus one may multiply any given utility function by an arbitrary positive number, and add or subtract a constant, without interfering with the properties of the function.[4]

MEAN-VARIANCE UTILITY FUNCTIONS

When the number of possible outcomes to a given action is large, the calculations needed to identify the action which yields maximum expected utility could become very cumbersome. Fortunately, there exists a wide range of situations in which the calculations can be very much simplified: situations in which it is not necessary to look at the whole range of possible outcomes but merely at the average or expected outcome and at the dispersion of possible outcomes about that average. The most appropriate measure of dispersion for our purposes is the variance of the distribution. (See page 133.)

Let us being by assuming that an individual's utility of wealth can be described (or approximated to a sufficient degree of accuracy) by a quadratic function (see the appendix to this chapter for a discussion of this):

$$U = a + bW - cW^2, \qquad (2.3)$$

where a, b and c are arbitrary constants, with b and c being strictly positive. These constants are the parameters which determine the exact shape of the function and so distinguish one individual's utility function from another's. Several such quadratic utility functions are illustrated in Figure 2.6 (p. 22).

The family of quadratic functions is sufficiently versatile that it is not unreasonable to assume that many people's utility functions may be approximated, at least over a certain range of wealth, by a quadratic function, choosing the most appropriate values for a, b and c.

A major drawback in the use of quadratic utility functions, however, is that for large enough levels of wealth they all eventually turn downwards at sufficiently high levels of wealth. The implication of this is that after a certain level of wealth has been reached, additional wealth actually imposes a disutility on the individual – the Midas syndrome! However, it is likely in practice that no possible outcome of any action open to the individual will take him into that region of the function.

The main advantage to be gained from the use of quadratic utility functions is that they allow considerable simplification in the calculation of expected utility. Consider the following situation. An individual is contemplating a certain course of action which has a large number of possible outcomes, each with its associated probability of occurrence (an outcome being defined as the resulting wealth of the investor subsequent to undertaking the action). The outcomes, together with their associated probabilities, are described by the probability density function in Figure 2.4.

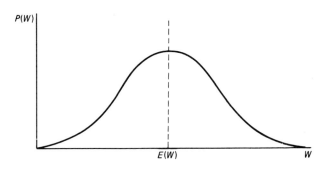

Figure 2.4

The mean or expected outcome is denoted by $E(W)$ and the variance of the distribution by $V(W)$. Let us assume that the individual who is contemplating the action has the quadratic utility function

$$U(W) = a + bW - cW^2. \qquad (2.4)$$

then, by the expected utility theorem, the utility of taking the action will be

$$E[U(W)] = E[a + bW - cW^2], \qquad (2.5)$$

which, since the expectations operator may be taken inside the brackets, becomes*

$$E[U(W)] = a + bE[W] - cE[W^2]; \qquad (2.6)$$

but

$$E[W^2] = (E[W])^2 + V[W], \qquad (2.7)$$

so, by substituting equation (2.7) into equation (2.6) we obtain

$$E[U(W)] = a + bE[W] - c(E[W])^2 - cV[W]. \qquad (2.8)$$

The implication of equation (2.8) is that, given a quadratic utility function, the utility of an action, the outcome of which is a random variable, depends solely upon the expected outcome $E[W]$ and the variance $V[W]$. It is not necessary to examine each possible outcome in turn.

INDIFFERENCE CURVES IN E–V SPACE

From equation (2.8) it is clear that the same level of utility may be achieved by a variety of combinations of $E[W]$ and $V[W]$. It is, in other words, possible to compensate for increased risk by a sufficiently large increase in expected wealth. The locus of all combinations of $E[W]$ and $V[W]$ which yield the same level of utility is said to form an *indifference curve* in *E–V* space.

The shape of such curves may readily be determined by fixing the level of expected utility in equation (2.8) at some arbitrary value $E[U]$, and rewriting the equation to bring $V[W]$ over to the left-hand side:

$$V[W] = \frac{a - E[U]}{b} + \frac{b}{c}E[W] - (E[W])^2. \qquad (2.9)$$

Equation (2.9) thus identifies all combinations of $E[W]$ and $V[W]$ which yield the same level of expected utility $E[U]$; it is, in other words, the equation of an indifference curve in *E–V* space. Different individual curves may be plotted by changing the value of $E[U]$

*See the Statistical Appendix, p. 133.

within the first term of the right-hand side of equation (2.9). Since this term is a constant one, $E[U]$ has been set, it is clear that such indifference curves are quadratic functions in $E[W]$. Several such indifference curves are illustrated in Figure 2.5, i.e. U_1, U_2 and U_3. U_3 represents a higher level of expected utility than does U_2, whi h in turn represents a higher level than does U_1.

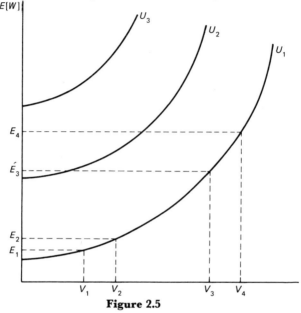

Figure 2.5

An important characteristic of indifference curves which have been derived from quadratic utility functions is that they all display the property known as *increasing marginal risk-aversion*. Thus, in order to compensate for increasing the level of risk by one unit from V_1 to V_2 (in Figure 2.5), one must increase expected wealth from E_1 to E_2. But as the individual bears more and more risk, the amount of necessary compensations for a unit increase in risk gets steadily larger, so that, for example, increasing risk by one unit from V_3 to V_4 requires a compensatory increase in expected wealth from E_3 to E_4, which is considerably greater than the increase from E_1 to E_2.

UTILITY FUNCTIONS IN RATE OF RETURN

So far the discussion of utility functions has been in terms of the utility of *wealth*. Once we know the utility of wealth, however, it is easy to infer the utility of income, since income is defined as the change in wealth. However, it is not usual to work with utility-of-income functions since a given level of income will generally give rise to different levels of utility, depending on the value of one's initial wealth.

For the purpose of applying utility theory to the problem of portfolio selection, we shall find it useful to modify the theory in such a way that we can base investment decisions on the concepts of 'expected rate of return' and 'variance of the rate of return' – rather than on expected terminal wealth and variance of terminal wealth.

The modification that we need requires us to establish that every quadratic utility-of-wealth function implies a corresponding utility of rate-of-return function which is unique for a given level of initial wealth (W_0).

The rate of return is defined as

$$r = \frac{W_T - W_0}{W_0} = \frac{W_T}{W_0} - 1, \qquad (2.10)$$

where W_0 is initial wealth and W_T is terminal wealth, which includes accrued dividends plus capital gains or losses.* For example, if one starts out with £20,000 and takes an action which has the consequence of transforming that sum into £25,000, the rate of return on that action is

$$r = \frac{25,000 - 20,000}{20,000} = 0.25. \qquad (2.11)$$

Note that 0.25 represents a rate of return of 25 per cent, *not* 0.25 per cent.

In order to make the necessary modification from utility of wealth to utility of rate of return, let us start out with the quadratic utility-of-wealth function

$$U = a + bW - cW^2, \qquad (2.12)$$

and let the decision-maker's initial wealth be given as W_0. A given action which transforms this sum into a terminal wealth of W_T will then yield the level of utility

$$U(W_T) = a + bW_T - cW_T^2. \qquad (2.13)$$

*In the theoretical structure developed here the existence of tax, and of differential tax rates on dividends and capital gains, is ignored. For practical implementation of the theory, all yields should be measured net of tax, where applicable.

In order to make the transformation we need to define three new parameters $a*$, $b*$ and $c*$:

$$c* = cW_o^2 \qquad \text{or } c = \frac{c*}{W_o^2} \qquad\qquad (2.14)$$

$$b* = bW_o + 2 \qquad \text{or } b = \frac{b* - 2}{W_o} \qquad\qquad (2.15)$$

$$a* = a + b* + c* \text{ or } a = a* - b* - c* \qquad (2.16)$$

Substituting for a, b and c in equation (2.13) above, we obtain:

$$U(W_T) = (a* - b* - c*) + \left(\frac{b* - 2}{W_o}\right)W_T - \left(\frac{c*}{W_o^2}\right)W_T^2 \quad (2.17)$$

which, on collecting terms, gives

$$U(W_T) = a* + b*\left\{\frac{W_T}{W_o} - 1\right\} - c*\left\{\left(\frac{W_T}{W_o}\right)^2 - 2\left(\frac{W_T}{W_o}\right) + 1\right\}. \quad (2.18)$$

However

$$\left(\frac{W_T}{W_o}\right)^2 - 2\left(\frac{W_T}{W_o}\right) + 1 = \left\{\frac{W_T}{W_o} - 1\right\}^2 = r^2. \qquad (2.19)$$

Consequently expression (2.18) can be rewritten as

$$U(W_T) = a* + b*r - c*r^2, \qquad\qquad (2.20)$$

which is a quadratic utility function in the rate of return r. Thus for every quadratic utility-of-wealth function, we can (contingent on the level of initial wealth) derive a unique corresponding utility of rate-of-return function. This latter function has one drawback, however, namely that the values of $a*$, $b*$ and $c*$ will change as the decision-maker's level of initial wealth changes – as may readily be verified from equations (2.14)–(2.16).

Conclusion

In this chapter we have been concerned with the development of a theory of rational decision-making under conditions of risk – where the outcome or consequence of an action is unknown at the time when the decision was taken. The general theory developed here will be applied in Chapter 6 to the specific problem of choosing an optimal portfolio of assets under conditions of uncertainty as to the future performance of these assets. However, in order to put that problem in perspective, we shall find it convenient to first develop two further related subject areas: (i) the theory of asset selection in a world where risk is totally absent; and (ii) the meaning of the term 'risk' in the sense in which it is used by economists and financial analysts. The exploration of these topics is undertaken in Chapters 3 and 4 respectively.

Appendix to Chapter 2: Quadratic Functions

Quadratic functions are functions which can be written in the general form:

$$Y = a + bX + cX^2, \tag{2.21}$$

where X and Y are the arguments, or variables, of the function, and a, b and c are the parameters, or coefficients, which distinguish one example of such functions from another.

When quadratic functions are plotted graphically the resulting graph is known as a parabola and looks broadly like either the dashed or solid examples in Figure 2.6. Parabolas have two general characteristics:

(i) They have only one turning-point, and consequently if they cut the X axis at all (they may not – see the dashed example), then they cut it twice – the values of X at which the axis is crossed are referred to as the roots of the equation.

(ii) As the value of X tends to either plus or minus infinity, the value of the function (i.e. Y) tends to either plus infinity (if c is a positive number), or to minus infinity (if c is a negative number).

Quadratic functions can take on a wide variety of shapes depending on the specific values given to a, b and c. Consequently when we know the values of a, b and c we can discover certain specific characteristics of the function in question:

(i) The value of a determines where the function crosses the Y axis. It is straightforward to establish this, since the function crosses the Y axis at the point $X = 0$. Setting X equal to zero in equation (2.21) results in $Y = a$.

(ii) The value of X at which the function changes direction (i.e. from being upward-sloping to downward-sloping, or vice versa) can readily be found by differentiating the function, setting the derivative equal to zero, and solving for X; thus

$$\frac{dY}{dX} = b + 2cX \qquad (2.22)$$

consequently

$$X = \frac{-b}{2c}. \qquad (2.23)$$

In this way, the value assigned to b helps to determine the turning-point of the function.

(iii) The function is symmetrical about its turning-point.

(iv) The two values of X at which the function cuts the X axis are given by the formula

$$X = \frac{-b \pm \sqrt{(b^2 - 4ac)}}{2c}, \qquad (2.24)$$

from which it is apparent that these will be real numbers only if the term inside the square-root sign is positive; that is if $b^2 \geqslant 4ac$.

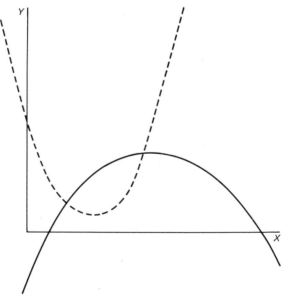

Figure 2.6

CHAPTER 3

The Theory of Asset Selection in the Absence of Risk

How does one define an 'asset'? What is it that distinguishes one object from another such that one of the pair may be termed an asset while the other may not? In everyday conversation the term *asset* is often used to denote an object which is desired or useful – as opposed to a *liability* which imposes an obligation on the owner, or which is possibly a nuisance.

This interpretation is unfortunately too loose for our purpose and we need to define a definition which pinpoints the essential characteristics of an asset. The first point to note is that assets come in a very wide variety: bonds, works of art, equity shares, house property, antiques, university education, loans made – all have one thing in common, namely that they may rightly be considered to be *assets*. The concept is thus very broad in scope encompassing both *financial* assets, such as bonds, equity and loans, and *real* or physical assets, such as house property and antiques.

The essential characteristic of all assets is that they generate a stream of income (either realised or potential) for their owner. Thus the equity-holder receives (uncertain) dividends and also capital appreciation/depreciation, the house owner receives rent, the antique-owner receives capital appreciation/depreciation, and so on.

Several points strike one immediately about this characterisation of an asset. In the first place, the income which an asset generates need not necessarily be positive. For example, if one purchases a painting for £4000 and on selling it one year later receives only £3000, the asset in question has generated an income of *minus* £1000. Thus if we define an asset as something which generates a stream of income (positive or negative), the everyday distinction between assets and liabilities becomes irrelevant: what was previously described as a 'liability' is now regarded as being simply an asset having a negative income stream. In a world of certainty it would be possible to know in advance whether a given object would generate a positive or a negative income, and consequently the everyday distinction between assets and liabilities could be maintained. However, in a world of uncertainty it is impossible to know in advance whether a given object will turn out to be an asset or a liability. Consequently it is customary to abandon the traditional distinction and to refer to all objects which generate income streams (positive or negative) as *assets*.

Second, the income generated may be notional (unrealised) rather than actual. Thus a block of equity shares, purchased at a particular time, may appreciate in value by £100 in the course of the following year, but this income is not realised unless the shares are sold at the end of the year. Consequently, if the block of shares, which was bought for, let us say, £500, is held for two years and then sold for £550, we may regard that as an asset which generated an income of £100 in the first year (unrealised) and generated an income of *minus* £50 in the second year (i.e. £550 − £600).

Last, an object may do more than generate an income stream. For example, being an art collector may, apart altogether from the income stream which the purchase of works of art generates, be in itself an enjoyable activity. Consequently one must be careful to distinguish the consumption component from the investment component when describing or characterising any asset.

Every asset can be abstractly, or formally, characterised by listing the net cash flow to which it gives rise in each period in time over its life span. Two assets which give rise to identical net cash-flow streams are, from our point of view, indistinguishable as assets, even though they may differ considerably in their physical attributes.

In such characterisations it is necessary to include the purchase cost of the asset at the time of acquisition and the amount realised at the time of sale, since the difference between the two is an essential component of the return on the asset. This way of describing an asset enables one to concentrate on the relevant financial characteristics of the asset without reference to its physical or institutional properties, which for the purpose of evaluating the asset are irrelevant.

A typical example of such a net cash flow stream is given below as

$$-10,000, \ -2000, \ 4000, \ 7000, \ 20,000.$$

This might, for example, represent an asset which was purchased for

£10,000 – possibly a lease on a shop – and which produced a net loss of £2000 in the first year, making profits of £4000 and £7000 in the second and third years respectively. The remainder of the lease was then sold for £20,000. The life of such an investment would be taken as four years.

Framework for Asset Selection

The essence of the problem of asset selection is that of choosing, on the basis of some criterion of desirability. a sub-set or portfolio of assets from among the vast if not infinite selection that is available. Such a choice must in general be made without exceeding the available supply of funds.

A special case of the above problem arises when one is offered a single asset and must either accept or reject the offer.

The existence of the two types of problem suggests the need for two separate, though related, criteria for asset selection. The first, the *ranking* criterion, provides the solution to the former more general problem, while the second, the *accept/reject* criterion, provides the solution to the latter problem.

Before any asset selection can be made, however, it is first necessary to provide a framework within which the available assets may be compared in a consistent manner. We shall find it convenient to begin by explicitly listing a set of assumptions which provides such a framework.

It is usual in situations such as this to begin with a list of somewhat restrictive assumptions, and to develop the basic theory on the basis of these. The next stage in the process is to relax these restrictive assumptions as much as possible and to explore the resulting modifications which must be made to the basic theory. There is unfortunately always an element of trade-off between the degree of realism in the assumptions and the simplicity of the resulting theory.

The initial set of assumptions are given below (those which will subsequently be relaxed are marked with an asterisk):

(1)* the whole of the income stream generated by each available asset is known with certainty from the outset;

(2) time is measured in *periods*, each of equal length (the chronological equivalent of a *period* – i.e. day, month, year, or whatever – is arbitrary and may be chosen by the investor as that which is most convenient for the analysis of the problem in hand);

(3) income accrues, if at all, only at the end of each period;

(4)* all assets under consideration have an equal life span, namely *T* time periods;

(5) all assets are independent, i.e. the return on any one asset does not depend on whether another is also undertaken or not;

(6)* the capital market is a perfect market, i.e. the interest rate at which money may be borrowed is the same as the rate at which it may be lent (note that we are not assuming here that any desired sum can in fact be borrowed);

(7) assets are infinitely divisible – this is equivalent to assuming that if one cannot afford to purchase the whole of an asset then one can purchase a share in it;

(8) no asset is available in unlimited quantity – thus, while it may be possible to purchase a chemist shop on the High Street, it is not generally possible to purchase fifty identical chemist shops on the same High Street.

The above eight assumptions serve to define a world of perfect certainty, free from risk. Such a world provides a starting-point for the theory of portfolio selection.

Portfolio selection must logically be preceded by the exercise of asset evaluation. In the following sections the most widely used criteria for asset evaluation are described, and the corresponding implied principles of portfolio selection are given.

NET PRESENT VALUE CRITERION (NPV)

The net present value criterion is based upon the consideration that any given sum of money which accrues at a specific date in the future may be translated into an equivalent sum in the present by appropriate *discounting*.

The concept of 'discounting' is a fundamental one in any discussion of intemporal financial transactions, and consequently it is essential that the rationale behind this concept be fully understood.

Suppose that you have £2000 that you wish to lend out for one year. You insist that the loan must be risk-free – in that you are guaranteed repayment at maturity – and you are aware that the going rate of interest for risk-free loans of this size† is 15 per cent; then you naturally would expect to receive £2300 back at the end of the year, £300

---

†The risk-free interest rate may vary with the size of the loan because of the economies of scale in administering larger loans.

being 15 per cent of £2000. This situation may be expressed as:*

$$£2000 + £2000 \times 0.15 = £2300 \tag{3.1}$$

or

$$£2000 \times (1.15) \qquad = £2300, \tag{3.2}$$

which is to say that £2000 *compounded* at 15 per cent for one year equals £2300.

Discounting is simply the same operation looked at from a different point of view. Suppose that you (now as a potential borrower) expect with certainty to receive £2300 in one year's time. How much money could you reasonably expect to borrow today on the strength of that £2300? Clearly, if the interest rate on riskless loans of that size was 15 per cent, a potential lender would be willing to loan you £2000 since he would then be receiving the market rate of interest on his capital. The £2000 is thus said to be the *present value* of £2300 and is found by discounting the sum in question (i.e. £2300) by one plus the market rate of interest, i.e.

$$\frac{£2300}{1.15} = £2000. \tag{3.3}$$

Clearly the time at which the sum of money is due to be received affects its present value. If, for example, the £2300 were not due to be received until two years hence, the potential lender would have his loan outstanding for two years and so would be willing to lend a sum of money, £X, determined by the consideration that the compounded value of £X over two years must equal the amount which he will be repaid, i.e. £2300. Thus

$$£X(1.15)^2 = £2300. \tag{3.4}$$

Consequently

$$£X = \frac{£2300}{(1.15)^2} = £1740, \tag{3.5}$$

so that the present value of £2300 accruing in two years' time is £1740.

It should now be clear that the principle of discounting may be extended in order to compute the present value of a sum of money which accrues at any moment in the future. Thus if S is the sum of

*Note that 15 per cent of a sum is equal to that sum multiplied by 0.15.

money, T is the number of time periods which elapse before it is due to be received, and r is the relevant rate of discount, the present value (PV) of the sum is given by

$$PV = \frac{S}{(1 + r)^T}. \tag{3.6}$$

Present values are additive, in that the present value of a stream of income is simply the sum of the individual present values of the components of the stream. Thus, pursuing the above example, if one expects to receive £2300 in one year's time and another £2300 in two years' time, the present value of that income stream is simply

$$PV = \frac{£2300}{(1.15)} + \frac{£2300}{(1.15)^2} = £2000 + £1740 = £3740. \tag{3.7}$$

In the light of the above discussion it is clearly a straightforward task to translate any income stream into its equivalent present value by the standard discounting procedure. In the case of an annuity (i.e. a uniform income stream which accrues in perpetuity), the calculation is particularly simple. Thus the present value of an income stream of £100 per annum (in perpetuity) is given by

$$PV = \frac{100}{(1 + r)} + \frac{100}{(1 + r)^2} + \frac{100}{(1 + r)^3} + \cdots \tag{3.8}$$

Multiplying both sides by $1 + r$, we obtain

$$(1 + r)PV = 100 + \frac{100}{(1 + r)} + \frac{100}{(1 + r)^2} + \cdots \tag{3.9}$$

Next, subtracting (3.8) from (3.9), we obtain

$$(1 + r)PV - PV = 100, \tag{3.10}$$

since remaining terms on the right-hand sides cancel out, i.e.

$$PV = \frac{100}{r}. \tag{3.11}$$

The present value of a positive income stream (i.e. a stream all of whose terms are positive) may legitimately be interpreted as the marketable value of that asset (i.e. the income stream). A negative element is essentially a debt which must be discharged in the future, its present value may be interpreted as that sum of money which, if set aside and invested today, will have accumulated sufficiently to discharge the debt when it falls due. When an income stream contains both positive and negative elements we may compute its net present value (*NPV*), which is simply the present value of the positive elements *minus* the present value of the negative elements. *NPV* may thus be regarded as the present value of the profit which the income stream represents – i.e. the excess of income over outlay.

Summing up, a project or investment which has a life span of T time periods and which generates an income stream of returns $S_0, S_1, S_2, \ldots, S_T$ (each of which may be positive or negative) will have a net present value given by the expression*

$$NPV = S_0 + \frac{S_1}{(1+r)} + \frac{S_2}{(1+r)^2} + \cdots + \frac{S_T}{(1+r)^T}, \quad (3.12)$$

or, more compactly†

$$NPV = \sum_{t=0}^{T} \frac{S_t}{(1+r)^t}. \quad (3.13)$$

Simple-profile Projects

An investment project will generally entail an initial outlay so, that S_0 and possibly some other S_ts will be negative. Similarly, if one is contemplating the purchase of an asset, S_0 being the purchase price, any immediate returns will invariably be negative. In addition, the investment project may at various points in its life entail expenditure (e.g. maintenance or replacements) which exceeds receipts in that time period, resulting in a negative S_t. Thus in some cases the sign pattern on the income stream might be an irregular mixture of pluses and minuses, e.g.

$$-, -, +, +, -, +, +, +. \quad (3.14)$$

We shall find it convenient in later discussions to have a term for investment projects in which only one sign change occurs, e.g.

$$-, -, -, +, +, +, +, +. \quad (3.15)$$

Such projects will be referred to as *simple-profile* projects.

*Since $(1+r)^0 = 1$ for all values of r, the first term on the right-hand side of (3.12) is written simply as S_0.

†Σ (pronounced 'sigma') is known as the summation operator and is simply a convenient means for expressing a sum of similar terms. It instructs the reader to sum a number of terms similar to the one which appears immediately after the sigma, in which the index t takes on the successive values 0, 1, 2, ..., T.

The use of NPV as a basis for asset selection gives rise to a number of related criteria, the most appropriate one depending on the nature of the problem.

Accept/reject criterion. Where only a single asset is being considered for possible acquisition, the NPV criterion is: accept (i.e. purchase) the asset if its NPV is positive; reject it if it is negative. Since the cost of purchase and all other dated outlays have been included in the calculation of NPV, a positive value of the latter may legitimately be interpreted as the present value of the profit which the asset generates. Hence an NPV of zero is the point which divides an *asset* from a *liability*, to use both those terms in their everyday sense.

Ranking criterion. A variety of possible situations exist in which the investor simultaneously evaluates a number of assets for possible purchase. In the simplest case all assets involve the same initial outlay, have the same life span, and generate non-negative income flows in every period except the initial period. If by S_{it} we denote the net income flow from the ith asset in the tth time period, the above situation may be described formally as

$$S_{10} = S_{20} = \ldots = S_{K0}, \tag{3.16}$$

where K is the number of assets under consideration, and

$$S_{it} \geqslant 0 \text{ for all } i, \text{ and for } t = 1, \ldots, T. \tag{3.17}$$

In the above situation the NPV criterion dictates that the investor lists, or ranks, the assets in descending magnitude of their NPVs, and, beginning at the highest, acquires assets with descending levels of NPV until his budget is exhausted. Since the present value of his total profit is simply the sum of the present values of the individual assets held, the above criterion will maximise the present value of the investor's total profit.

In the case where not all of the assets involve the same initial outlay (i.e. where (3.16) does not hold), but where (3.17) continues to hold, the above criterion requires slight modification. A valid measure of the rate of profit, or rate of return, on an asset is its NPV divided by the sum of money required to acquire it, S_{i0}. Since the investor's object is assumed to be the maximisation of the rate of return on his capital, investment projects requiring unequal capital outlays should be ranked on the basis of descending values of

$$\frac{NPV_i}{S_{i_0}}, \tag{3.18}$$

where NPV_i is the NPV of the ith asset.

Here, as before, the investor should, starting with the highest, acquire the assets in descending order until his budget is exhausted. This policy will produce the highest rate of return on the investor's wealth.

In the third and most general case, in addition to the assumption of unequal initial outlays, no restrictions are placed on the signs of S_{it}, i.e.

$$S_{it} \gtrless 0 \text{ for all } i \text{ and for all } t. \tag{3.19}$$

Here the NPV criterion requires yet a further modification. In this case the investor's outlay is not necessarily all made at the initial point in time, but different projects may require supplementary outlays at different points in time. Expressions (3.20) and (3.21) illustrate the sign patterns of two such projects:

$$-, -, +, +, + \tag{3.20}$$

$$-, +, +, -, + \tag{3.21}$$

Here it would clearly be inappropriate to deflate the NPVs by S_{i_0} since S_{i_0} is no longer a valid measure of financing the ith project. Instead, one should deflate NPV_i by $\hat{S}_i$, where $\hat{S}_i$ is defined as the present value of all elements in the income stream having negative signs. It is thus the present value of the cost of financing the ith project. Having ranked the projects on the basis of

$$\frac{NPV_i}{\hat{S}_i}, \tag{3.22}$$

the investor acquires the assets in the usual way until his budget is exhausted.

THE NPV CURVE AND RELATED CRITERIA

Nothing has been said as yet about the most appropriate discount rate to use in NPV calculations. This is a matter which is relatively straightforward to resolve theoretically but which can give rise to certain practical complications. The basic principle to follow is that the discount rate used should reflect the opportunity cost of the sum being discounted. Thus in a perfect capital market in which a single interest rate rules there is no problem, for that interest rate reflects both the cost of borrowed funds and the rate of return obtainable on money lent.

In practice, however, a discrepancy will often exist between the rate at which funds may be borrowed and the rate at which they may be lent. In such circumstances it would appear to be more sensible to incorporate both rates in the *NPV* calculation, depending on whether the net cash flow in a given time period is positive – in which case it may be lent – or negative – in which case it must (in general) be financed by borrowing. (It is convenient to postpone further discussion of this particular issue until pp. 44–5.)

Varying the discount rate used in the *NPV* calculation will naturally result in different estimates of the *NPV* of a given income stream. Such estimates may be plotted against the rate used in deriving them, and for simple-profile projects such a graph will resemble that in Figure 3.1.

Two other investment criteria, which are related to *NPV*, can also be identified in Figure 3.1.

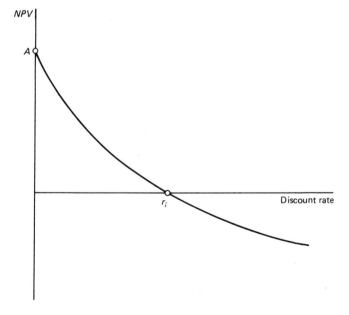

Figure 3.1

ACCOUNTING NET PROFIT (ANP)

The accounting net profit of an investment project is simply the undiscounted sum of the elements in the net cash-flow stream, or, what amounts to the same thing the NPV with a zero discount rate – corresponding to point A in Figure 3.1.

However, while the ANP is easy to compute, it is virtually useless as a reliable investment guide, the reason being that it takes no account of the time profile of the cash-flow stream, and consequently ignores the cost of time.

While, for all positive discount rates, any project which has a negative ANP (i.e. is unprofitable on that measure) will also have a negative NPV, it does not follow that a positive ANP implies a positive NPV. The investment project

$$-100, 50, 60 \tag{3.23}$$

has a positive ANP but is clearly unprofitable if the cost of financing it is, say, 12 per cent. Thus it is possible that a project which is considered profitable on the ANP criterion fails to break even on the NPV criterion.

INTERNAL RATE OF RETURN (IRR)

The internal rate of return is a widely used measure of the innate profitability of an investment. Its intuitive appeal may be seen in the following single-period example. The investment

$$-100, 118 \tag{3.24}$$

represents an immediate outlay of £100, followed by a net cash inflow of £118 in one year's time. It is patently clear that the profitability of this investment is 18 per cent (or 0.18). What is not so immediately obvious, however, is that if we use the rate of profitability as the appropriate discount rate in computing the NPV of (3.24), we shall get an NPV of zero!

$$NPV = -100 + \frac{118}{1.18} = -100 + 100 = 0. \tag{3.25}$$

On reflection this should not be surprising since the NPV is a measure of the excess return on the investment over and above the cost of financing it. Consequently, if we replace the market rate of interest with the investment's own rate of profitability, we should expect to get an NPV of zero.

It follows that if one can identify that discount rate which reduces the *NPV* of a project to zero, one has identified the internal rate of return on the project in question. The discount rate in question is denoted by r_i in Figure 3.1.

The *IRR*, like the *NPV*, is thus a measure of the rate of profit on an investment project, and consequently the implied criteria for asset selection based on the *IRR* measure are similar to those described above based on the *NPV* measure.

Accept/reject criterion. Since the market rate of interest, r, represents the opportunity cost of the funds used to purchase the investment project, and since the rate of profit generated by that project is its internal rate of return, r_i, it follows that if the latter exceeds the former the funds used in acquiring the project are earning a higher rate of return than their opportunity cost and so the project should be accepted. Otherwise it should be rejected.

Ranking criterion. Where more than one project is being considered, all the projects should be ranked in descending order of their *IRR*, and, starting with the highest, acquired in descending order until one's budget is exhausted. This policy will ensure the highest average rate of profit (as measured by the *IRR*) on the investor's capital.

Consider next the two-period investment project

$$-100, 60, 60. \tag{3.26}$$

How can one calculate the *IRR* of this project? What is required is a value of r which will satisfy the equation

$$0 = -100 + \frac{60}{(1+r)} + \frac{60}{(1+r)^2}. \tag{3.27}$$

A slight notational change will simplify matters somewhat. Let

$$\frac{1}{(1+r)} = D, \tag{3.28}$$

where D is now referred to as the *discount factor*. Consequently

$$\frac{1}{(1+r)^2} = \left\{\frac{1}{(1+r)}\right\}^2 = D^2, \tag{3.29}$$

and in general,

$$\frac{1}{(1+r)^t} = D^t. \tag{3.30}$$

Equation (3.27) may now be rewritten as

$$0 = -100 + 60D + 60D^2, \tag{3.31}$$

which is a straightforward quadratic equation in D. This may be solved analytically, by applying the formula (2.24), to yield the solutions:

$$D = 0.884, \text{ or } D = -0.0066. \tag{3.32}$$

Inserting these values for D in equation (3.28), we obtain the internal rates of return:

$$r = 13.1 \text{ per cent, or } r = -153.1 \text{ per cent.} \tag{3.33}$$

The presence of multiple solutions, such as the above, forms one of the inherent difficulties in the use of the internal rate of return as an investment selection guide. In the first example above (expression (3.24)), which covered only one time period, there was only one *IRR*. In this latest example, which covers two time periods, there are two competing *IRR*s. In general, when the investment project stretches over T time periods, there will be T *IRR*s. The reason for this is that the calculation of the internal rate of return involves finding the solution to a Tth degree polynomial equation in D, and Tth degree polynomials have T roots, or solutions.

Fortunately things are not as bleak as they seem. In the first place, not all T roots will necessarily be different, repeated roots being a possibility. Second, not all of the T roots will necessarily be real numbers. Some may be imaginary numbers (such roots always occur in pairs) and these may safely be ignored. Last, since the asset-selection criteria involve a comparison between the *IRR* and the market rate of interest, we will generally be concerned with those roots in the vicinity of the latter. Figure 3.2 illustrates the above situations. Here there are four roots: D_1, being negative, corresponds to a negative value of r_i; D_2 and D_3 represent a pair of complex roots; while D_4, if less than unity, represents a positive value of r_i.

Descartes's Rule of Signs

An important theorem, due to Descartes, states that *the number of positive real roots of a polynomial is equal to the number of changes in sign of the coefficients, minus an even non-negative number.*

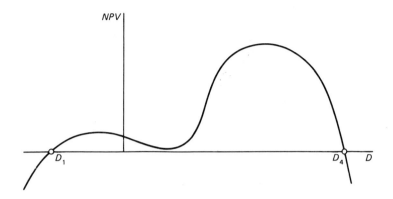

Figure 3.2

A sign change occurs whenever the elements of the income stream change from positive to negative, or vice versa. Thus the following investment project has three sign changes (identified by asterisks) and hence it has at most three real roots in D:

$$-250, * 50, 150, * -60, * 200, 200 \qquad (3.34)$$

Of particular interest to us is the number of real roots in D which lie between $D = 0$ and $D = 1$. The reason for this concern is that since $D = 1/(1 + r)$, the value $D = 1$ implies that $r = 0$, and similarly $D = 0$ implies that r is infinitely large. Thus the existence of a unique real root in D lying between 0 and 1 implies that there is a corresponding unique positive internal rate of return on the project. We now establish a sufficient condition for the existence of such a unique positive *IRR*. (We shall find it convenient to use the expression $P(D)$ to denote a polynomial whose variable is D.)

Any polynomial of the type

$$P(D) = \sum_{t=0}^{T} S_t D^t, \qquad (3.35)$$

where the coefficients $S_t < 0$ for all $t = 0, \ldots, M$, and $S_t > 0$ for all $t = M + 1, \ldots, T$, has a unique positive root. This may be established as follows. If it has a positive root, that root is unique (by Descartes's rule of signs) since there is only one sign change.

That it *has* a positive root is established by noting that the value of the polynomial, evaluated at $D = 0$, is S_0, which, by assumption, is negative, and that as D increases in value the final terms, which have positive coefficients, will dominate the sign of the expression. Consequently there exists some positive value of D, say D^*, at which $P(D^*) = 0$, and so D^* is the required unique positive real root of the polynomial.

Since if $P(D^*) = 0$, then, by the above argument, $P(\tilde{D}) > 0$ for all $\tilde{D}$ such that $\tilde{D} > D^*$. From this it follows that if we require the unique positive real root to be not greater than some value, say $\tilde{D}$, then it is necessary that $P(\tilde{D}) \geqslant 0$. In particular, for the root to be less than unity we require that

$$P(1) = \sum_{t=0}^{T} S_t > 0, \qquad (3.36)$$

where $\sum_{t=0}^{T} S_t$ is a familiar concept, namely the Accounting Net Profit (ANP).

Thus in conclusion a sufficient condition for a simple-profile project to have a unique positive internal rate of return is that its accounting net profit be positive.

Computation of the Internal Rate of Return

The actual calculation of *IRR* involves solving an equation of the general form:

$$0 = c_0 + c_1 D + c_2 D^2 + \ldots + c_T D^T, \qquad (3.37)$$

where $c_0, c_1, \ldots, c^T$ are constants, or coefficients.

In the case where $T = 1$, the equation is linear and the solution is trivial. Similarly, where $T = 2$, the equation is quadratic and the application of the formula (2.24) yields the two roots. Unfortunately, however, there is no general formula for solving polynomial equations for arbitrary values of T. In order to find a solution to such equations one must resort to *iterative* methods. An iterative method consists of taking an arbitrary initial guess at a solution value (i.e. a value of D which sets the right-hand side of (3.37) equal to zero); calculating the discrepancy between the value of the right-hand side and zero; and using some rule for improving one's initial guess, making use of the discrepancy as a guide. This process is then repeated, using the improved value as the new 'initial guess', until the discrepancy becomes so small that it can be ignored – i.e. until the desired degree of accuracy has been reached.

One of the most widely used techniques for solving polynomials is the *Newton approximation formula*, described next. Suppose that we wish to find a value of D which will solve equation (3.37) (i.e. make the right-hand side equal to zero). Let the expression $P(D^*)$ denote the value of the right-hand side when the variable D is given the value D^*. Similarly, let the expression $P'(D^*)$ denote the value of the first derivative† of the right-hand side when D is given the value D^*. To use the Newton approximation technique, first choose an arbitrary initial value of D, denoted by D_1, and then update that value to D_2 according to the iteration rule:

$$D_2 = D_1 - \frac{P(D_1)}{P'(D_1)}. \qquad (3.38)$$

This updating procedure is next repeated to get the next approximation, D_3:

$$D_3 = D_2 - \frac{P(D_2)}{P'(D_2)}. \qquad (3.39)$$

The successive applications of this iteration rule will generate a sequence of approximations – D_1, D_2, ..., D_K – to a solution, or root, of the equation, the values of D_K getting successively more accurate as the series continues. When two successive values of D_K stabilise to sufficient decimal places, the iterative procedure may be terminated, and the current value of D_K taken as a solution of the equation.

Numerical example. A numerical example may help to clarify matters further. Consider the problem of finding an internal rate of return for the investment

$$-150, -20, 100, 100. \qquad (3.40)$$

What we are seeking is a value of D which satisfies the equation

$$0 = -150 - 20D + 100D^2 + 100D^3. \qquad (3.41)$$

In the above notation, $P(D)$ and $P'(D)$ are now defined as

$$P(D) = -150 - 20D + 100D^2 + 100D^3 \qquad (3.42)$$

†The first derivative of (3.37) is
$$P'(D) = c_1 + 2c_2D + 3c_3D^2 + \ldots + Tc_TD^{T-1}.$$

and

$$P'(D) = \quad -20 \quad +200D \quad +300D^2 \qquad (3.43)$$

Since the polynomial equation (3.41) is of third degree, there are three internal rates of return to this project. However, a casual inspection of the figures in (3.40) would suggest that there should be an *IRR* somewhere in the region of 10 per cent and this is the one that we wish to converge on; if there also happened to be a root of, say, -95 per cent, that root would not be of any interest to us since the project is plainly profitable. The question is: how profitable?

We take as our initial guess the value $D = 1.0$. This implies an *IRR* of zero, which, though patently a bit low, makes the arithmetic for the first iteration very simple! The details of the successive iterations are provided in Table 3.1. Using the value $D = 1$ we compute $P(1)$ from (3.42), which is 3; $P'(1)$ from (3.43), which is 48;

Table 3.1

*Calculation of internal rate of return**

Iteration number, i	D_i	$P(D_i)$	$P'(D_i)$	D_{i+1}
1	1.0	3.0	48.0	0.9375
2	0.9375	0.153808	43.117187	0.933933
3	0.933933	0.000494	42.845585	0.933922
4	0.933922	0.000022	42.844749	0.933921
5	0.933921	0.000000	42.844709	0.933921

and by applying the Newton approximation formula (3.38), we arrive at an improved estimate of $D = 0.9375$. Using this new estimate, we next repeat the procedure, calculating $P(0.9375)$ and $P'(0.9375)$ and applying the formula to get an even more improved estimate of $D = 0.933933$. The process stops when two successive estimates agree to a sufficient number of decimal places.

The final value of $D = 0.933921$ corresponds to an internal rate of return of 7.08 per cent on the project.

What of the two remaining roots? Since the project is a simple-profile one and has a positive accounting net profit, we know from page 37 that it has a unique positive *IRR*. For the purpose of illustra-

*For ease of calculation, expression (3.41) can be divided through by ten without affecting the result.

tion, however, the graph of (3.42) is illustrated in Figure 3.3. Since it only cuts the horizontal axis once, only one of its roots is real, the other two being imaginary numbers.

Where the life span of a project is long, the computation of the *IRR* by hand can be quite a tedious undertaking. The appendix to this chapter contains a short computer programme which will extract the internal rate of return for projects with a life span of up to thirty years. It is simple to use and will repay the investment of the short amount of time needed to master it.

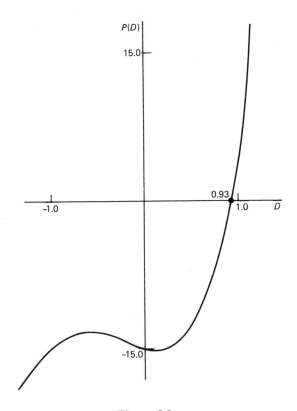

Figure 3.3

Finding further solutions. Any polynomial of order T can be written in factorised form as

$$0 = (D - R_1)(D - R_2) \ldots (D - R_T), \qquad (3.44)$$

where R_1, R_2, ..., R_T are the roots, or solution values, of the equation. For example, the polynomial

$$0 = -2 - 11D + 295D^2 + 150D^3 \qquad (3.45)$$

may be rewritten in factorised form as

$$0 = (D - 0.1)(D + 2)(D + 0.066). \qquad (3.46)$$

Setting D $= -2$ in (3.46) will make the middle term equal to zero, and hence the whole expression equal to zero. Since (3.46) is identical to (3.45) (multiply out the former to check that you get the latter), setting $D = -2$ will thus make the right-hand side of (3.45) equal to zero, and so is a root of the equation. By an identical argument it may be demonstrated that $D = 0.1$ and $D = -0.066$ are the two other roots of (3.45).

What we have accomplished in the previous section has been to find one of the Rs. The particular one which we find will depend on our initial guess, of course. Having found one, we could simply take another arbitrary initial guess and attempt to discover another root. This would be computationally inefficient, however, for we cannot be sure that we would not arrive back at a root that we had already identified. This possibility becomes more likely as the number of roots remaining to be identified gets smaller.

The correct way to go about obtaining the remaining roots is to reduce the order of the polynomial by extracting the root already obtained. Thus if we identify a root, which we shall term the Tth root, and since the ordering of the roots is purely a matter of convenience, we can divide the polynomial through by $D - R_T$ to obtain a new polynomial of order $T - 1$:

$$0 = (D - R_1)(D - R_2) \ldots (D - R_{T-1}), \qquad (3.47)$$

containing only those roots from the original equation which are yet to be identified. We can then apply the Newton approximation technique to the simplified system.

This procedure has two advantages for finding successive roots: first, it reduces the arithmetic involved since one is continually working with lower-order polynomials; and second, it safeguards us against the possibility of discovering the *same* root several times on occasions where it only occurs once.

NET TERMINAL VALUE (NTV)

The final approach considered here to the problem of asset evaluation lies in computing the net terminal wealth to which the asset would give rise. Whereas with the NPV criterion each element in the income stream was discounted to the present, using the NTV criterion each element is *compounded* to the terminal date. Thus all costs are compounded to the terminal date, and subtracted from the sum of compounded returns (all intermediate returns are thus implicitly assumed to be invested at the market rate of interest). The difference between the two measures the net addition to wealth which accrues to the investor as a result of under taking the project.

Continuing to assume the existence of a perfect capital market in which funds can be borrowed and lent freely at a common interest rate, say 10 per cent, consider the investment project having a four-year life span:

$$-1000, 100, -300, 800, 1000 \qquad (3.48)$$

The total financing cost of this investment, compounded to the terminal date, consists of £1000 borrowed for four years (£1464.1), and in addition £300 borrowed for two years (£363). The gross terminal returns consist of £100 compounded at 10 per cent for three years (£133.1), £800 compounded for one year (£880), and of course the £1000 which accrues at the end of the final time period and so is not compounded at all. The difference between the sum of compounded returns, £2013.1 (i.e. £133.1 + £880 + £1000), and the compounded costs, £1827.1 (i.e. £1464.1 + £363), represents the net terminal value of the investment, namely £186.

The reader may object that the initial £1000 does not have to be financed for the whole four years but may be repaid as the positive net cash flow becomes available. However, this objection is irrelevant as long as the assumption of equal borrowing and lending rates is maintained. The reader may verify for himself that repaying the borrowed capital at the rate at which positive cash flows become available and investing the residue at the market interest rate (10 per cent) will produce the same figure for net terminal value, namely £186. The distinction does become important, however, as soon as the assumption of a perfect capital market is dropped, and this aspect of the problem is explored in the next section on imperfect capital markets.

An interesting formal relationship exists between the concepts of net terminal value and net present value: in a perfect capital market the latter is by definition equal to the former discounted to the present at the market rate of interest. This may easily be demonstrated:

$$NTV = S_0(1 + r)^T + S_1(1 + r)^{T-1} + \ldots + S_T. \quad (3.49)$$

Dividing both sides by $(1 + r)^T$, we get

$$\frac{NTV}{(1 + r)^T} = S_0 + \frac{S_1}{(1 + r)} + \ldots + \frac{S_T}{(1 + r)^T} = NPV. \quad (3.50)$$

In the above example, the net present value of the investment is obtained as

$$NPV = \frac{NTV}{(1 + r)^T} = \frac{186}{1.10^4} = \pounds127.04. \quad (3.51)$$

Here again it is left as an exercise to the reader to verify that £127.04 is in fact the net present value of the investment, calculated in the conventional manner of page 29.

It is also worth noting that since $1/(1 + r)^T$ is a constant for any discount rate, r, there is a one-to-one relationship between the NPV criterion and the NTV criterion in that any project which is accepted on the basis of its NPV would also have been accepted on the basis of its NTV. Similarly, the ranking of projects under the NPV criterion will be exactly the same as their ranking under NTV.

Accept/reject criterion. Accept a project if its NTV is positive; reject it if it is negative.

Ranking criterion. The same principles determine the ranking of projects on their NTV as on their NPV. Thus in the simplest case, described formally by (3.16) and (3.17), the projects are ranked simply on the basis of their NTVs and, starting with the largest NTV, are acquired in descending order until one's budget is exhausted.

In the next case, where (3.17) continues to hold but (3.16) does not, each NTV should be deflated by that project's S_0 since it is the rate of terminal profit rather than its absolute amount which should determine the ranking. In this case the projects will be ranked on the basis of

$$\frac{NTV_i}{S_{i_0}}, \quad (3.52)$$

where NTV_i is the NTV of the ith project, and S_{i_0} is the initial element in the income stream of the ith project.

Last, in the case where neither (3.16) nor (3.17) holds (i.e. where (3.19) holds) each NTV_i should be deflated by the total compounded cost of financing the project. Thus, let S_i be the sum of the compounded values of the negative elements in the ith income stream, then the ranking should be carried out on the basis of

$$\frac{NTV_i}{S_i}. \tag{3.53}$$

INVESTMENT APPRAISAL IN IMPERFECT CAPITAL MARKETS

The time has now come to drop the assumption that the interest rate at which money can be lent is the same as that at which it can be borrowed. The former will now be denoted by r_l and the latter by r_b. We shall also assume that r_l is less than r_b.

Once the principles of discounting and compounding have been assimilated, however, it will be seen that dropping the assumption of a perfect capital market merely makes the arithmetic involved somewhat more burdensome. The following example illustrates the process. Consider the investment project

$$-500, 300, 373, -198, 800 \tag{3.54}$$

Let us assume as before that the cost of borrowing capital is 10 per cent, but now the rate of interest obtainable on invested funds is assumed to be only 8 per cent. In this case it is clearly optimal to repay the borrowing as quickly as the cashflow position will allow, and the calculation of NTV proceeds on that basis. The actual calculations, which are self-explanatory, are set out in Table 3.2.

Table 3.2

NTV calculation in imperfect capital market

Time period t	Net value at beginning + of period	Interest paid $(-)$/ + received $(+)$	S_t	=	Net value at end of period
0	—	—	-500		-500
1	-500	-50	300		-250
2	-250	-25	375		100
3	100	8	-198		-90
4	-90	-9	800		$701 = NTV$

The net value at the end of the final time period is the NTV of the project. It is the addition to the investor's net wealth which is attributable to this project. Not surprisingly, the NTV in this case is less than would have been the case had the capital market been perfect and with both rates of interest at 10 per cent.

What of the NPV measure in an imperfect capital market? Bearing in mind that the NPV is simply today's borrowing equivalent of the profit which the project generates, it may be found directly by applying formula (3.50) to the NTV figure of £701 to obtain £479. Note that since we are talking about the borrowing equivalent, r_b is the appropriate interest rate to use in the discounting formula (3.50).

One important consequence of an imperfect capital market is that it now becomes necessary to distinguish between those projects which are internally financed (i.e. without the necessity of obtaining a loan) and those which are financed by borrowing. In the former case, in using one's own wealth to acquire an asset, the opportunity cost of the funds employed is simply the interest forgone on them, namely r_l. Since it is not necessary to borrow externally, the borrowing rate r_b is irrelevant, and the computation of NTV (or NPV) is carried out in the same way as in the perfect capital market case using r_l as the appropriate interest rate.

PROJECTS WITH UNEQUAL TIME HORIZONS

The fact that one undertakes a four-year project having an NTV of £186 does not mean that one has to wait for four years before consuming any of the profit which the project generates. The very concept of NTV is based on the consideration that if one did abstain for the four years one would have £186 to spend. However, the concept of NPV is based on the alternative consideration that if one desired to consume at the outset all of the profit generated by the project, the amount available for consumption would be its NPV, i.e. £127.04 in this case.

Alternatively one might wish to consume a constant amount in each of the four years. If a sum of money £X is borrowed at the beginning of each of the four years and all loans are repaid at the completion of the project, the amount which can be consumed annually out of an NTV of £186 is determined by the equation

$$X(1.10)^4 + X(1.10)^3 + X(1.10)^2 + X(1.10) = 186, \quad (3.55)$$

i.e.

$$X = £36.5. \quad (3.56)$$

Consider next the case of an investor who wishes to choose one of the three mutually exclusive projects *A*, *B* and *C*, whose characteristics are as follows:

Project	Life span (years)	NTV ($£$)
A	3	150
B	2	100
C	5	175

Initially, let us assume a perfect capital market where the interest rate is 10 per cent. Although project C has the highest NTV, this figure is somewhat deceptive since it does not accrue until five years hence. If the investor were to select project *A* and invest the £150 NTV for a further two years at the market rate of 10 per cent, he would have accumulated £181.5 at the end of five years – so on that basis *A* is to be preferred to *C*. If we look at the five-year implication of choosing project *B* (and investing the £100 NTV for the remaining three years), we see that its five-year NTV is £133, so it remains the least desirable of the three. Summarising, then, if we take the five-year horizon as our bench-mark, project *A* is the most preferred of the three. A little reflection should convince the reader that taking three years, or two years, as the bench-mark would leave the ranking of the projects unaltered – since that would be tantamount to taking the three-year, or two-year, $NPVs$ of the five-year $NTVs$.

In a perfect capital market, then, it is only necessary to take all projects to a common reference point in time in order to rank them correctly.

When the capital market is imperfect the situation becomes more complicated. Now it is no longer the case that the choice of project is independent of one's desired consumption pattern. A variation on the last example will serve to illustrate the nature of this interdependence. Let us continue to assume that the borrowing rate is 10 per cent but now we shall assume that, due to capital-market imperfection, the lending rate is only 7 per cent. The investor, as before, wishes to choose one of the three mutually exclusive projects *A*, *B* or *C*.

In order to avoid unnecessary computational complications, we shall also assume that the three projects are of the *point-input/point-*

output type – which is to say that one lays out all the capital required in the initial time period and no returns accrue until the final time period. Formally the cash-flow stream has the following sign pattern:

$$-, 0, 0, \ldots, 0, +. \tag{3.57}$$

The net value of each of the three projects may be plotted as a function of time, as in Figure 3.4, from which the reader can see that, while project B is always dominated by the other two, the choice between projects A and C depends upon the time when the comparison is made. Project A is initially superior to C – that is to say, if the investor has a short horizon and wishes to consume his wealth early, he will do best by choosing A. However, if he is prepared to wait until about the fourth year before consuming his wealth, then project C will provide the higher consumption opportunity. In other words, the comparative evaluation of projects A and C is *not* independent of the moment when the individual wishes to consume his wealth. This result is a direct consequence of the discrepancy between borrowing and lending rates.

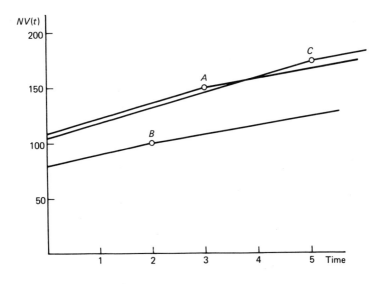

Figure 3.4

Appendix to Chapter 3

The following FORTRAN computer programme identifies a root of the Tth degree polynomial $P(D)$, using Newton's Approximation, in the neighbourhood of the initial value of D. The initial value used below is $D = 1.0$, which may be changed by the user by appropriately altering the twelfth line. The maximum degree of the polynomial is thirty, which may be increased if necessary by inserting the value $T + 1$ in the first statement. The array $A(\;\;)$ contains the $T + 1$ coefficients of the polynomial. $P(D)$ and $P'(D)$ are evaluated by Horner factorisation.

```
      REAL  A(31)
      INTEGER  T
      READ  (5,1) T
1     FORMAT (I2)
      M = T + 1
      READ (5,2) (A(I), I = 1,M)
2     FORMAT (10F8.2)
      WRITE (6,3) T
3     FORMAT (31H THE DEGREE OF THE POLYNOMIAL
     IS, I4)
      WRITE (6,4) (A(I), I = 1,M)
4     FORMAT (29H THE  COEFFICIENTS  OF  P(D)  ARE,
     //(10F12.2/))
      D = 1.0
      DO 7 1 = 1,100
      P = A(M)
      N = M−1
      DO 5 K = 1, N
      J = M−K
5     P = P*D + A(J)
      Q = T*A(M)
      N = M−2
      DO 6 K = 1, N
      J = M−K
      KK = J−1
6     Q = Q*D + KK*A(J)
      SD = D
      D = D − P/Q
      TEST = ABS((D − SD)/SD)
      IF(TEST.LT.1.0E-5) GOTO 8
```

```
 7  CONTINUE
    GOTO 10
 8  R = (1.0 − D)*100.0/D
    WRITE (6,9) R
 9  FORMAT (//38H THE RATE OF RETURN ON THIS
    PROJECT IS, 2X,F6.2, 9H PER CENT)
    GOTO 12
10  WRITE (6,11)
11  FORMAT (122H THIS PROBLEM HAS FAILED TO
    CONVERGE IN 100 ITERATIONS. IF LONGER RUN
    REQUIRED, INCREASE THE LAST FIGURE IN THE
    THIRTEENTH LINE)
12  CONTINUE
    STOP
    END
```

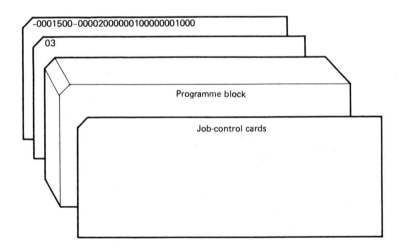

Figure 3.5 *Sample input*

OUTPUT FOR THE ABOVE SAMPLE INPUT
THE DEGREE OF THE POLYNOMIAL IS 3
THE COEFFICIENTS $P(D)$ ARE

$$-15.00 \qquad -2.00 \qquad 10.00 \qquad 10.00$$

THE RATE OF RETURN ON THIS PROJECT IS 7.08 PER CENT

CHAPTER 4

The Nature of Risk

The theory developed in Chapter 3 is applicable only in situations where the outcome of an investment decision is known with certainty. In some real-life situations this may be a not-inappropriate approximation to reality – for example, where the investment is of short duration and promises specific returns to the investor. However, in the majority of investment problems the outcome of any given decision may at best only be guessed at. The investor may be able to specify a range of possible outcomes, and possibly attach a probability to each, but beyond that it may not be possible to go. In such situations the investor is involved in decision-making under conditions of risk or uncertainty, and the purpose of this chapter is to develop a frame of reference within which it is possible to analyse and quantify the concept of risk.

The term 'risk' is used in this book as a blanket term to denote a variety of situations in which the outcome of an action cannot be foretold with certainty. The first such situation arises where the outcome is a random variable with a readily identifiable probability density function (see the Statistical Appendix, p. 133, for a definition of probability density function). For example, if one tosses two coins simultaneously, the possible outcomes are: (i) no heads appear; (ii) one head appears; or (iii) two heads appear; and the associated probabilities of these outcomes are 0.25, 0.5 and 0.25 respectively. A situation such as this, in which the decision-maker is able to identify all of the possible outcomes and attach a probability to each, is defined as a condition (or situation) of *risk*.

In the example just given the probability attached to each outcome was its *objective* probability – that probability which could be deduced from the logic of the situation without reference to the views of the decision-maker. There is no compelling reason, however, why any individual decision-maker has to accept the figures 0.25, 0.5 and 0.25

as being the respective probabilities of the three possible outcomes. For some mood or sentiment best known to himself any given decision-maker might refuse to accept these objective figures and choose to regard each of the three possible outcomes as equally likely. He may, in other words, use his *subjective* assessment of the probability of each outcome as a basis for decision-making. This situation would also be described as a 'condition of risk', and indeed for the development of portfolio theory we require no more than that the individual be able to specify a subjective probability density function on the range of possible outcomes for each of his actions.

The final alternative to a condition of certainty that we shall consider here is the situation where the individual is unable to attach any probability, objective or subjective, to the possible outcomes of his action. This situation is often described as being one of *uncertainty*, as opposed to risk.[1] In this latter case we shall follow conventional practice and invoke the *principle of insufficient reason*, which asserts that if an individual is unable to attach specific probabilities to the possible outcomes of an action, he must regard them all as being equally probable. This approach has the effect of subsuming this last case into the framework of the 'subjective probability' situation described above.

In all that follows, then, the terms 'risk' and 'uncertainty' will be used interchangeably, and will refer to the situation where the decision-maker is at least able to attach subjective probabilities to each of the possible outcomes of his action – whether by recourse to the principle of insufficient reason or not.

In everyday language the term 'risk' has a much broader meaning than that which attaches to it in portfolio theory. We talk, for example, of the risk involved in crossing a busy street or driving on a motorway, and in most situations it is extremely difficult to classify – let alone quantify – the specific types of risk involved. Fortunately the varieties of risk encountered in the domain of finance and investment are fairly well-defined and relatively easy to classify. The four major categories of risk with which we shall be concerned are: (i) purchasing-power risk; (ii) default risk; (iii) income risk; and (iv) capital risk.

Purchasing-power Risk

The act of investing involves not just the surrendering of a given sum of money for a specific length of time but, more importantly, it involves forgoing the consumption of real goods and services which that monetary sum would finance. At the end of, say, a five-year investment the investor may be pleased to see that his initial money outlay has doubled, but his satisfaction will be short-lived if he subsequently finds out that prices have trebled over the same period, so that the *real purchasing power* of his final wealth is less than that which he surrendered, or postponed, five years previously.

Economists, ever conscious of this potential confusion, maintain a clear distinction between *nominal* and *real-valued* variables – the latter being simply nominal figures deflated by the current price level.

Any investment which is not index-linked to future price levels exposes the investor to purchasing-power risk – this being the risk that changes in the price level will erode or eliminate any nominal return on the investment. In such a situation an investment which appears profitable and attractive in nominal terms might not be half as appealing in real terms after changes in the purchasing power of money have been taken into account.

However, purchasing-power risk does not present any significant problems for the theory of asset selection – for the following reason. The theory of asset selection is primarily concerned with comparing different assets and choosing the most desirable from the available set. It does not make any difference whatsoever whether the relevant calculations are all carried out in nominal terms or all in real terms – the conclusions of the theory will be identical. Where purchasing-power risk is important, however, is in resolving the logically prior problem as to what proportion of one's wealth to consume now and what proportion to delay consuming until some time in the future. This latter problem is described by economists as the '*consumption-saving*' problem and should not be confused with the subject-matter of this book, which is the 'portfolio-selection' problem.

In other words, the appropriate time to take account of purchasing-power risk is when deciding whether to invest or not. However, having once made the decision as to how much wealth to invest, the comparison between the alternative available securities will not be affected by the level of purchasing-power risk.

Default Risk

Default risk arises whenever the investor (or creditor) has reason to believe that the debtor will default on either the interest payment, or the capital repayment, or both. Banks and other lending institutions usually take an explicit view of default risk by charging differential rates of interest according to the customer's credit rating. Institutions which have a large number of accounts, for example credit-card companies, can predict with a fairly high degree of accuracy the likely loss through default and so can estimate the interest loading to place on all accounts so as to ensure any given (net of default) return.

Capital Risk and Income Risk

These two types of risk are best analysed together because they are closely related concepts. They both arise as a consequence of the failure of the investor to match the maturity of his assets with the maturity of his liabilities. If his assets have longer to go to maturity than his liabilities, then he is exposed to capital risk; if shorter, he is exposed to income risk, as we shall see. In order to explore the nature of capital and income risk, however, we first need to digress slightly in order to see the relationship between the price of a long-term bond and the rate of interest.

Let us begin by looking for a formal definition of a 'bond'. For our purposes a bond may be considered as a promise to pay the bearer the sum of £1 per annum in perpetuity. Note that it is *not* a promise to pay a given percentage of anything but rather a nominal sum of money. How then does this definition of a bond relate to securities such as $3\frac{1}{2}$ per cent War Loan? If $3\frac{1}{2}$ per cent War Loan was originally sold for £100 and if the bond paid £3.50 to the holder per annum, then this would represent a $3\frac{1}{2}$ per cent rate of return to the holder on his £100. However, should he decide to sell the bond in February 1977, he would not receive £100 for it but a mere £28, this being the going market price for $3\frac{1}{2}$ per cent War Loan at that time. The person who bought it for £28 would continue to receive £3.50 per year interest payment, but this would not represent a rate of return of $3\frac{1}{2}$ per cent to him but rather a rate of return of 12.5 per cent on his outlay of £28. In this case the bond would continue to be referred to, for historical reasons, as $3\frac{1}{2}$ per cent War Loan but its yield would be 12.5 per cent.

From the theoretical point of view, then, it would be more appropriate to consider one unit of $3\frac{1}{2}$ per cent War Loan as being equivalent to three and a half bonds, each paying £1 per annum in perpetuity.

When it comes to selling a bond the price that can be obtained may be interpreted as the purchaser's estimate of the present value of the income stream to which the bond gives rise. What is the present value of an infinitely long income stream of £1 receipts? It is simply

$$P = \frac{1}{(1+r)} + \frac{1}{(1+r)^2} + \frac{1}{(1+r)^3} + \cdots \qquad (4.1)$$

Multiplying both sides of equation (4.1) by $1 + r$ gives

$$(1+r)P = 1 + \frac{1}{(1+r)} + \frac{1}{(1+r)^2} + \cdots \qquad (4.2)$$

Next, subtracting equation (4.1) from (4.2) gives

$$rP = 1, \qquad (4.3)$$

since all of the remaining terms on the right-hand side cancel out. Equation (4.3) may be rewritten as

$$P = \frac{1}{r}, \qquad (4.4)$$

which asserts that the market value of a bond is the reciprocal of the rate of interest. Thus if the rate of interest is 9 per cent, the market value of a bond (as we have defined a bond) will be $1/0.09 = £11.1$. If the interest rate subsequently increases to 14 per cent, the market value of the bond will fall to $1/0.14 = £7.1$. The relationship in equation (4.4) between the current rate of interest and the price of a bond holds strictly true only for bonds with an infinite life span. For all finite-life bonds there will be a remainder term of $1/(1+r)^n$ left over when equation (4.1) is subtracted from (4.2). However, where the bond is a long one (i.e. where n is a large number) the effect of this term will be trivial and can be ignored.

With this background to the relationship between the price of a long-term bond and the rate of interest, we now return to the analysis of the concepts of 'capital risk' and 'income risk'. These concepts can best be explained by means of a numerical example.

NUMERICAL EXAMPLE

Let us assume that Mr Smith incurs a liability to Mr Jones in that Smith receives from Jones a lump sum of £1000 on condition that he repays Jones the sum of £5604 in twenty years' time. This contract represents to Jones a rate of return on his initial wealth of 9 per cent.

The most conservative investment policy that Smith could pursue under these circumstances would be to match the maturity of his liability (i.e. twenty years) with a higher-yielding, default-free asset of the same maturity – say a 10 per cent government bond having twenty years to run to maturity. This course of action would guarantee Smith a profit (assuming that intermediate dividends, if any, could be reinvested at 10 per cent) of £1123 on expiry of the contract – this being the difference between £1000 compounded at 10 per cent over twenty years (£6727) and Smith's liability to Jones of £5604.

However, in the event of a suitable twenty-year bond not being available, Smith must either invest the £1000 in a bond of longer maturity, selling it at the current market price after twenty years when his liability falls due, or a bond of shorter maturity, with the intention of reinvesting for the remainder of the twenty-year period when the short-dated bond matures. The former course of action exposes Smith to capital risk, as we shall see, and the latter to income risk.

Suppose that Smith invests the £1000 in a bond of fifty years maturity which, though it pays no intermediate dividends, has a redemption price* of £117,391. This is equivalent to an annual yield of 10 per cent over the fifty years. The bond in question is assumed to be readily marketable and completely free of default risk. Thus Smith anticipates no difficulty in selling it at the end of the twenty-year period for a sum of money £X, which, accumulated (or compounded) at the rate of interest prevailing in twenty years time, would amount to £117,391 over the remaining thirty years of the life of the bond.

Suppose next that over the course of the twenty years for which Smith holds the bond the level of interest rates changes such that when he comes to sell it the market rate of interest is, say, 13 per cent. Whoever purchases the bond from Smith at the end of the twenty years will do so on the understanding that he will receive £117,391 in a further thirty years. The sum of money which, compounded at 13 per cent, accumulates to £117,391 in thirty years is £3001 – which

---

*This somewhat artificial bond is used in the example in order to sidestep the cumbersome arithmetic involved if one were to take account of reinvesting yearly dividends. It does not affect the nature of the conclusions to be drawn from the example.

is as much* as Smith could reasonably expect to receive for the bond. In this case he ends up with a loss of £2603 on the contract! – all because of a three-point change in interest rates and his failure to match the maturity date of his asset with that of his liability. Such is the essence of capital risk.

The other side of the coin of course is that if Smith had successfully anticipated a fall in interest rates over the twenty-year period, to, say, 7 per cent, then the market price of the fifty-year bond after twenty years would have been £15,421, thereby giving him a profit of £9817 on the contract.

What if Smith had chosen the second course of action and purchased a security with less than twenty years to run to maturity? Let us assume that he purchased a ten-year bond with similar characteristics to the one described above and having a redemption price of £2594 – which once again represents an implicit yield of 10 per cent. Assume also that over the course of the first ten years the level of interest rates falls from 10 per cent to, say, 7 per cent. This fall in interest rates implies that when the first bond matures at the end of ten years Smith will only be able to reinvest the resulting £2594 at 7 per cent for the second decade, thus giving him a final sum of £5103 – insufficient to pay Jones £5604. This is the essence of income risk.

The corollary here is that a rise in interest rates at the end of the first decade would have enabled Smith to make a substantial profit on the reinvestment of the £2594 – something which would not have been possible had he been locked in to the fifty-year bond, which would have suffered a capital loss as a consequence of any rise in the interest rate.

Summing up, we can see that if an investor is unable (or does not wish) to match the maturity of his asset with that of his liability, then if he expects a rise in interest rates before his liability matures he should invest in the short term, even though this exposes him to income risk, while if he expects a general fall in interest rates he should invest in the long term, even though this exposes him to capital risk. The two types of risk are thus very closely related.

One further type of investment policy remains open to the investor

---

*Let £X be the sum of money which a purchaser would be willing to pay for the bond, given that similar bonds are yielding 13 per cent. Then it follows that £$X(1.13)^{30}$ = £117,391. Solving for X gives us X = 117,391/$(1.13)^{30}$ = 117,391/39.116 = £3001.

who does not wish to expose himself to either capital or income risk, and that is to put part of the £1000 in the fifty-year bond and the rest in the ten-year bond. If he followed such a strategy his objective would be, in the event of a rise in interest rates, to compensate for the capital losses incurred on the long bond by the added interest income obtained by the reinvestment of the proceeds of the short bond. On the other hand, in the event of a fall in interest rates, this policy would hope to provide sufficient capital gains on the long bond to compensate for any loss of income incurred by having to reinvest the proceeds of the short bond at a lower interest rate. This type of investment policy is known as the *immunisation* of the investment fund, and its effect is to safeguard, or immunise, the investor simultaneously against the adverse effects of capital risk and income risk.

In what proportion should the investor split his £1000 between long and short bonds so as to immunise his fund against a three-point rise in interest rates? The necessary calculations are quite simple. £1000 invested long would produce a loss of £2603, whereas if invested short would produce a gain of £3202. This latter figure means that it is only necessary to invest £813 in short bonds to produce an interest gain of £2603 which would match the capital loss of the same amount resulting from investing £1000 in long bonds. Thus it follows trivially that the ratio in which the fund should be split between long and short bonds is 1000/813, or, in other words, £552 in long bonds and £448 in short. Such an investment policy would have the effect of completely immunising the investor against a three-point rise in interest rates.

The question naturally arises as to whether the same split between long and short bonds would also fully immunise the investor against a fall of three points in the interest rate. The answer, which the reader may easily work out, is that it would not. The capital gains resulting from investing £552 in long bonds would be £5419 and are offset by the income loss of £224 on the short bond investment, giving an over-all profit of £5195 as a result of the three-point interest rate fall. In this latter case the placing of £448 in short bonds may be thought of as an insurance by the investor against the possibility that his anticipation of a fall in the interest rate was erroneous. In other words he surrenders part of the profit that he would receive if his anticipation of a fall in interest rates proved correct in order to reduce the loss that he would make should it prove erroneous. The effect on final profit of moving from a 100 per cent investment in long bonds to a

55.2 per cent investment is illustrated in Figure 4.1. The curve labelled 100L illustrates the relationship between final profit and final interest rate on the assumption that 100 per cent of the £1000 is invested in long bonds. Similarly, the 55.2L curve illustrates the same relationship on the assumption that the fund is split 552/448 between long and short bonds. Similar curves may be constructed for any ratio in which long and short bonds could be split.

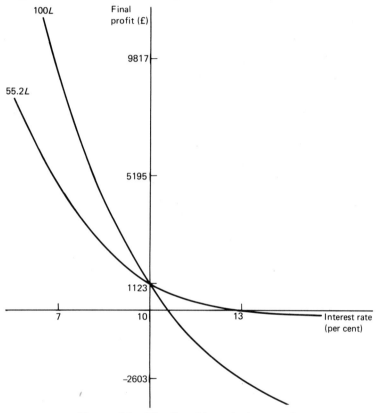

Figure 4.1   *The effect of immunisation on profit*

The Measurement of Risk

Although we have now defined the major categories of risk encountered, it is not sufficient to have merely a qualitative classification of risk – it is necessary in addition to be able to quantify the amount of risk inherent in any given investment project. The theory of portfolio selection under conditions of risk can only be made operational by using a measurable concept of risk, and it is to the task of providing such a measure that we turn next.

The most widely used measures of risk may best be explained by means of the previous example, which explored the difference between capital and income risk. Continuing with the above example, consider the various courses of action which are open to Mr Smith. In order to keep the example tractable, we will continue to assume that there are only two bonds available to him – a fifty-year bond and a ten-year bond. Smith may invest the whole £1000, or any proportion of it in the fifty-year bond – investing the remainder in the ten-year bond with the intention of reinvesting the proceeds of the latter in a further ten-year bond when it matures, at the rate of interest prevailing in ten years' time. Let λ be the proportion of the £1000 that Smith invests in the long bond and $1 - \lambda$ be the proportion that he invests in the short bond. Since λ can take on any value from zero to unity, Smith has an infinity of investment options open to him, each with its own expected level of profit and associated level of risk – as we shall see.

Consider, first, how Smith might formally summarise the level of risk involved in investing the whole £1000 in the fifty-year bond. The current rate of interest is 10 per cent. Smith's profit depends upon the market rate of interest in twenty-years' time – a random variable about which he will, of necessity, have some views (if only in that he considers all rates to be equally likely!). A hypothetical assessment by Smith of the likelihood, or probability, of various interest rates ruling at the end of twenty years is given in Figure 4.2.

Once Smith has purchased the fifty-year bond, the sole determinant of his profit or loss on the contract with Jones is the interest rate which pertains at the end of the twenty-year period. It is then a simple matter to calculate the profit or loss accruing to Smith as a consequence of each possible interest rate, and this is done in row 4 of Table 4.1. Each possible profit/loss may then be weighted by Smith's estimate of its likelihood of occurrence (which is, of course, his estimate of the probability of occurrence of the particular interest rate which generates the profit/loss). These calculations are carried out in Table 4.1 and illustrated in Figure 4.3, which is a visual representation of the likelihood of the possible outcomes resulting from the investment of the whole £1000 in the fifty-year bond. Figure 4.3 tells us that Smith's *expected profit* on the contract, under this investment policy, is £1308, which is the mean value, or the expected value, of the probability distribution of profit illustrated.

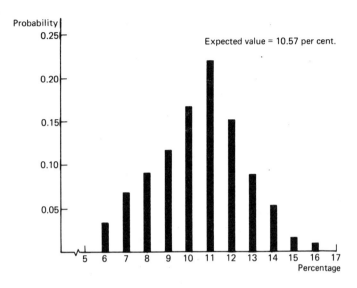

Figure 4.2   *Probability distribution of interest rates in twenty years' time*

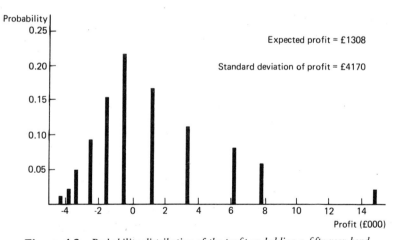

Figure 4.3   *Probability distribution of the profit on holding a fifty year bond*

If all possible outcomes having non-zero probabilities of occurrence

Table 4.1

Calculation of expected profit on the purchase of a fifty-year bond

(1) Market interest rate in twenty years' time (r per cent)	6.0	7.0	8.0	9.0	10.0	11.0	12.0	13.0	14.0	15.0	16.0
(2) Probability of occurrence	0.03	0.06	0.08	0.12	0.17	0.22	0.15	0.09	0.05	0.02	0.01
(3) Market value of thirty-year bond when interest rate is r per cent (£000)	20.4	15.4	11.7	8.8	6.7	5.1	3.9	3.0	2.3	1.8	1.4
(4) Smith's profit on the contract = (3) − 5.6 (£000)	14.8	9.8	6.1	3.2	1.1	−0.5	−1.7	−2.6	−3.3	−3.8	−4.2
(5) Profit weighted by probability = (4) × (2)	0.444	0.588	0.488	0.384	0.187	−0.011	−0.255	−0.234	−0.165	−0.076	−0.042

Expected profit = £1308 (expected profit is found by summing the elements of row 5).
Variance of profit = 17.40 (£000)^2.
Standard deviation of profit = £4170.

are bunched very close to the mean value of £1308, then the investment involves very little risk, since the investor can say with a high degree of accuracy what the final level of profit will be. Conversely, if there are outcomes substantially below the mean which have a significant probability of occurrence, then the investor is being exposed to the risk of occurrence of these adverse outcomes. This consideration has led to the convention that some measure of dispersion of the probability density function would be an appropriate measure of the degree of risk attached to a particular investment policy. There are many ways of measuring the dispersion of a probability density function. The measure most favoured by statisticians is the variance*, or equivalently its square root, the standard deviation. There is a one-to-one relationship between variance and standard deviation; consequently, as measures of dispersion, they are equivalent. A small variance implies that the distribution is closely grouped about the mean value, and that consequently one can predict the final profit with a fair degree of accuracy. Conversely, a large variance implies a high degree of uncertainty, in the sense that very little confidence can be attached to the actual outcome being close to the mean value. There is, in other words, a fairly high probability that the actual outcome will differ significantly from the mean value if the variance is large.

However, the variance is not the only measure of dispersion which can be applied to a probability density function. Alternative measures (which are defined in a technical sense in the Statistical Appendix, p. 136) are the range, the semi-interquartile range, and the mean absolute deviations (*M.A.D.*). Markowitz argues that when we talk about measuring risk we are primarily concerned with outcomes *below* the mean, since it is only these outcomes which are undesirable.[2] This suggests yet another measure of risk – the semi-variance – which is defined as

$$\sum_{i=1}^{k} p_i (r_i^* - E[r])^2,$$

where r_i^* refers only to those outcomes which are below the mean $E[r]$, and p_i is the probability of r_i^*.

The almost universal preference of statisticians for the variance (or standard deviation) as the most appropriate measure of dispersion

*See the Statistical Appendix, p. 133, for definitions of the various measures of dispersion.

stems from the fact that the variance alone, unlike all of the alternative measures proposed, is readily amenable to mathematical (or analytical) manipulation; that is to say, one can use the concept of variance as a building block in the development of portfolio theory and, by appropriate mathematical manipulation, derive specific formulae for the solutions of particular problems. Because of the relatively cumbersome ways in which the alternative risk measures are defined, they are not amenable to the same straightforward analytical manipulation as is the variance.

An additional reason why the variance is preferred as a risk measure to the semi-variance is that when the probability density function is symmetric – and there is strong evidence that this condition holds in the majority of cases with which we shall be concerned – then the semi-variance and the variance are identical as risk measures, the semi-variance in this case being literally half the value of the variance. Under such circumstances, then, there is nothing to be gained by abandoning the useful analytical flexibility of the variance measure in favour of the semi-variance.

In this book we shall follow the standard practice among portfolio theorists and settle on the variance as the most appropriate measure of the risk, or dispersion, attached to any given probability density function. Thus, reverting to the numerical example, the consequences to Smith of investing the whole £1000 in the fifty-year bond may be adequately summarised by the two parameters of the distribution in Figure 4.3, and Table 4.1, namely the expected profit of £1308 and the variance of profit of 17.40 (£000)^2. Since the units of measurement of the variance are not pounds but pounds-squared, many people prefer to use the square root of the variance as the measure of dispersion. In the above example, this would be £4170. Since there is a one-to-one relationship between the variance and the standard deviation, it clearly makes no difference which of the two we use as our measure of risk.

The question naturally arises as to whether the first two moments of a distribution, its mean and variance, are sufficient to summarise the distribution for the investor. The next highest moment, the third, is used as a measure of the skewness of the distribution, a zero value of the third moment indicating that the distribution is symmetric, as in Figure 4.4(i), a positive value that it is skewed to the right (i.e. has a fat right-hand tail), as in Figure 4.4(ii), and a negative value that it is skewed left, as in Figure 4.5(iii).

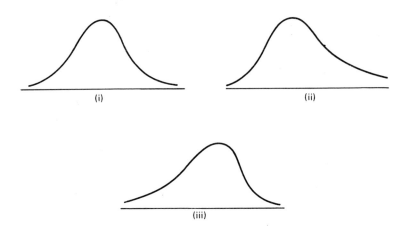

Figure 4.4 *Skewed distributions*

It is quite plausible that certain investors would not be indifferent as between the distributions shown in Figure 4.4(i) and 4.4(ii) even if both had the same mean and variance. The distribution shown in Figure 4.4(ii), while it has an increased probability of outcomes slightly below the mean, has a very small probability of outcomes which are a long way below the mean. An investor might well be willing to accept this trade-off and so prefer the distribution shown in Figure 4.4(ii) to the distribution shown in Figure 4.4(i). Do we then need to take account of the third moment? Most of the work in this field has not taken account of the third moment for a variety of reasons, the principal one being that most of the distributions which arise in the application of portfolio theory are in fact symmetric,[3] or at least nearly so. This is partly due to the fact that investors are typically involved in evaluating combinations of assets (portfolios) rather than single assets, and so there is a well-known statistical tendency for their sum to be symmetrically distributed even if the distributions of the individual assets are asymmetric.

Another reason why the third moment is not often used is that, as we have seen in Chapter 2, an investor with a quadratic utility function will not be influenced by it. His only concern will be with the mean and variance. If it is felt desirable to include the third moment in the analysis, however, this is easily accomplished. Instead of the utility function

$$U = a + bW + cW^2$$

which is quadratic, we simply substitute the cubic utility function

$$U = a + bW + cW^2 + dW^3$$

and rework the algebra on pages 15–18. The reader is invited to do this as an exercise.

CHAPTER 5

The Theory of Asset Selection under Conditions of Uncertainty

In Chapter 3 we explored the principles of asset selection in the absence of risk, and in the following chapter we examined the nature of risk as it applies to the characteristics of assets. The next step is to explore the theory of asset selection where the returns on the assets in question áre subject to some degree of risk. In this case the actual return on each asset will be a random variable since it will depend, in general, on uncertain events which may or may not occur in the future.

Whereas the theory elaborated in Chapter 3 was a multi-period theory, in that it could be applied to assets of any life span, we shall find it convenient to confine our attention in this chapter to the single-period theory of asset selection, postponing the multi-period aspects of the theory until Chapter 8.

This is not as great a limitation as it might at first appear, however, since the term 'period' is used in quite a different sense here. In Chapter 3 the length of a period was primarily determined by accounting convenience. For example, whereas the net rental income of a block of flats might be calculated as £12,000 per year, there is no reason other than that of relative convenience why it should not be specified as £1000 *per month* and calculations (*NPV*, *IRR*, or whatever) carried out using a month as the basic period – using monthly rates of interest of course! It follows trivially that the number of periods in the life span of the investment would have been twelve times greater if the latter course had been adopted.

In this chapter, however, the length of a period is determined by quite a different consideration. The essence of a *single-period* framework is that the investor does not have the option of, or does not intend, revising the composition of his portfolio between the moment he selects it (t_0) and the moment he liquidates it (T) in order to consume his wealth. The interval between t_0 and T is thus the length of the single period.

If he does wish to revise the composition of his portfolio, it is necessary to divide up the interval between t_0 and T into a number of periods in such a manner that any revisions which are desired may only be made at the beginning of a period. Here again the length of a period is primarily a matter of convenience.

In the theory of risk-free asset selection no reference was made to the problem of revising one's portfolio of assets. This is as it should be, since the portfolio, if initially optimal, will remain so indefinitely – due to the absence of risk. However, in the theory of risky-asset selection this is not the case and the problem of revising one's portfolio is an integral part of the over-all problem. It is for this reason that Chapter 8 is devoted to a discussion of the theory of portfolio revision while the basic or single-period theory is presented here.

Asset Universe and Data Requirements

The number of assets which are available for purchase is virtually infinite, and in undertaking any exercise in asset selection, we must therefore confine our attention to a specific set of assets and ignore all the others if the problem is to prove tractable. This set is known as the *asset universe*. There may be any number of assets in the asset universe and we shall typically deal with the general case where the number of assets is simply N. A collection of assets from within this set constitutes a *portfolio* and the theory upon which such a selection is based, is consequently referred to as the 'theory of portfolio selection'.

The first step in portfolio selection is to assemble the basic data on all assets in the asset universe. These data consist of the forecasts of the expected rates of return, over the single time period in question, for each of the N assets, the N variances and the $N(N-1)/2$ covariances* between each pair of assets. This represents a substantial volume of statistical information which grows more than proportionately with the size of the asset universe. In Chapter 6, however, we examine ways in which the basic model may be simplified so as to reduce significantly the amount of statistical input which is required.

Having assembled the above information, one is now in a position to proceed with the primary task of selecting an optimal portfolio

*Readers unfamiliar with the concept of covariance should consult the Statistical Appendix, p. 136.

having regard to one's own objectives and, specifically, one's attitude towards risk.

SINGLE-ASSET PORTFOLIOS AND DOMINANCE

We begin by examining the simplest of all possible portfolios, namely those consisting solely of a single asset. It is a straightforward matter to plot the expected return and standard deviation* of each such portfolio in $E - S$ space since these are simply the expected returns and standard deviations of the single component assets. Such an exercise is illustrated in Figure 5.1.

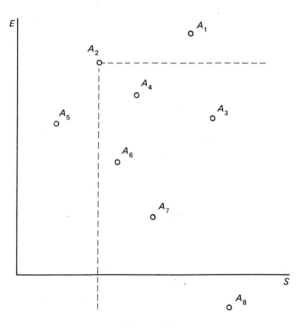

Figure 5.1

We have assumed in this example that there are eight assets, labelled $A_1, A_2, \ldots, A_8$, in the asset universe. It is evident from the diagram that A_8 is, for a risk-averter, the least desirable of all – having the lowest expected return (which is actually negative) and

---

*For reasons which will be clear later, it is more convenient to work with the standard deviation, which is the square root of the variance, rather than with the variance itself.

the highest degree of risk. Equally clearly, A_1 is unambiguously preferable to A_3 (having a higher expected return and a lower standard deviation), and, for the same reason, A_2 is preferable to A_3, A_4, A_6, A_7 and A_8, while A_5 is always preferred to A_6, A_7 and A_8.

Thus at the outset we can confine our attention to three of the eight (single-asset) portfolios, namely A_1, A_2 and A_5. All other portfolios are said to be *dominated*. A portfolio is said to be dominated when there exists an alternative feasible portfolio having the same or less risk combined with a higher expected rate of return, or – what amounts to the same criterion – having the same or higher rate of return combined with less risk. The concept of dominance is illustrated in Figure 5.1 by the dashed lines, A_2 dominating all portfolios in the lower right-hand quadrant.

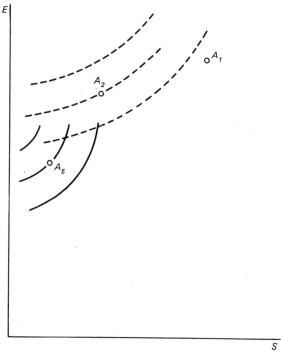

Figure 5.2

However, there is no objective way of choosing between the remaining three undominated portfolios. The choice of an optimal portfolio is confined to these three since all others are dominated by them, but the portfolio chosen depends upon the utility function, and more specifically the risk-aversion of the investor. This is illustrated in Figure 5.2, where the investor whose utility function generates indifference curves represented by the three solid ones maximises his utility by choosing A_5, whereas another investor, having a lesser degree of risk-aversion, has a utility map represented by the dashed lines and maximises his utility by choosing A_2.

RISK REDUCTION THROUGH DIVERSIFICATION

We consider next the problem of selecting an optimal portfolio where the portfolio may consist of either one or two assets. In order to illustrate such portfolios in E–S space we must first derive the formulae which enable us to express their expected returns and standard deviations.

The rule for deriving the expected rate of return for such portfolios is very straightforward and is based on the following fundamental theorem concerning means:

The expected value (i.e. the mean) of a weighted sum of random variables is the same weighted sum of their individual expected values.

A portfolio consisting of two risky assets may be thought of as a weighted sum of two random variables since the (random) rate of return on the portfolio is a weighted sum of the *(random)* rates of return of the two component assets, the weights being the proportions in which they are held.

Thus if the two assets in the portfolio have expected rates of return of E_1 and E_2 respectively, and if the proportion of total wealth invested in the first asset is w_1, with w_2 (which by definition is equal to $1 - w_1$) invested in the second, then the expected rate of return on the portfolio will be

$$E_p = w_1 E_1 + w_2 E_2, \qquad (5.1)$$

which, on substituting $1 - w_1$ for w_2, may be rewritten as

$$E_p = w_1(E_1 - E_2) + E_2. \qquad (5.2)$$

Thus the calculation of the portfolio's expected return is a very straightforward procedure. The calculation of the portfolio's standard deviation is slightly more complicated, however.

In order to derive the portfolio's standard deviation we make use of the standard statistical formula for expressing the variance of a combination of random variables – bearing in mind that the variance is the square of the standard deviation:

Let P *be a linear combination of the random variables* $X_1, X_2, \ldots, X_N$, *where the weights are* $w_1, w_2, \ldots, w_N$, *then the variance of this combination may be expressed as*

$$V_p = \sum_{i=1}^{N} \sum_{j=1}^{N} w_i w_j C_{ij}, \tag{5.3}$$

where C_{ii} *is the variance of the* i*th random variable and* C_{ij} $(i \neq j)$ *is the covariance between* X_i *and* X_j.

In our particular example, since the number of assets is two, this reduces to

$$V_p = w_1^2 C_{11} + w_2^2 C_{22} + w_1 w_2 C_{12} + w_2 w_1 C_{21}. \tag{5.4}$$

Recalling that C_{11} is simply the variance of the first asset (i.e. V_1), similarly for C_{22}, and that by definition $C_{12} = C_{21}$, the above expression may be simplified to

$$V_p = w_1^2 V_1 + w_2^2 V_2 + 2w_1 w_2 C_{21}, \tag{5.5}$$

which states that the variance of the two-asset portfolio is a weighted combination of the component-asset variances and of the covariance between them.

The covariance term in the last expression plays a crucial role in the theory of portfolio selection, for it is the medium through which the investor can reduce the over-all risk of his portfolio by appropriate asset diversification.

The correlation coefficient between two random variables (see the Statistical Appendix, p. 136), ρ, which is defined as

$$\rho = \frac{C_{12}}{S_1 S_2}, \tag{5.6}$$

can vary in value between minus one and plus one. This has implications for the covariance between the two variables. Specifically

$$\rho = +1 \quad \text{implies that } C_{12} = S_1 S_2$$
$$\rho = 0 \quad \text{implies that } C_{12} = 0$$
$$\rho = -1 \quad \text{implies that } C_{12} = -S_1 S_2$$

In order to see how C_{12} contributes to the reduction in the portfolio's variance, we next look at the three cases listed above.

Case One: Perfect Positive Correlation

If the returns on both assets are perfectly positively correlated, then we can make the substitution $C_{12} = S_1 S_2$ in equation (5.5) to give us

$$V_p = w_1^2 S_1^2 + w_2^2 S_2^2 + 2 w_1 w_2 S_1 S_2 \qquad (5.7)$$

$$= (w_1 S_1 + w_2 S_2)^2, \qquad (5.8)$$

i.e.

$$S_p^2 = (w_1 S_1 + w_2 S_2)^2 \qquad (5.9)$$

or

$$S_p = w_1 S_1 + w_2 S_2. \qquad (5.10)$$

Equation (5.10) states that in this case the standard deviation of the portfolio is simply the weighted sum of the standard deviations of the two component assets.

Combining equations (5.2) and (5.10) one can readily establish that the locus of all possible combinations of expected return and standard deviation of return arising from portfolios obtained by combining the two assets A_1 (having characteristics E_1 and S_1) and A_2 (having characteristics E_2 and S_2) is the straight line $A_1 A_2$ in Figure 5.3. This is shown in the following way. Equation (5.10) may be rewritten as

$$S_p = w_1(S_1 - S_2) + S_2, \qquad (5.11)$$

from which it follows, by rearranging, that

$$w_1 = \frac{S_p - S_2}{S_1 - S_2}. \qquad (5.12)$$

Substituting this value for w_1 into equation (5.2), and rearranging, gives us

$$E_p = a + b S_p, \qquad (5.13)$$

where

$$a = E_2 - \frac{S_2(E_1 - E_2)}{S_1 - S_2} \qquad (5.14)$$

and

$$b = \frac{E_1 - E_2}{S_1 - S_2}. \qquad (5.15)$$

Equation (5.13) is clearly that of a straight line, and is illustrated in Figure 5.3. It is important to remember that this result depends critically on the assumption that the returns on both assets are perfectly positively correlated.

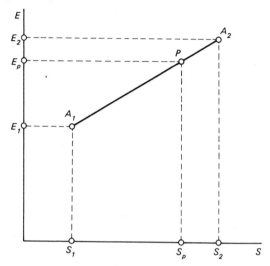

Figure 5.3

Case Two: Zero Correlation

If the realised rates of return on both assets are completely independent then the correlation between them is zero, which by definition implies that the covariance between them C_{12} is also zero. In this case equation (5.5) may be rewritten as

$$V_p = w_1^2 S_1^2 + w_2^2 S_2^2. \tag{5.16}$$

In order to find the weights – denoted by w_1^* and w_2^* – which generate the portfolio with the least risk, we substitute $1 - w_1$ for w_2 in equation (5.16) and set the derivative of that expression equal to zero, solving for w_1^*; thus

$$V_p = w_1^2 S_1^2 + (1 - w_1)^2 S_2^2 \tag{5.17}$$

$$= w_1^2 S_1^2 + (1 - 2w_1 + w_1^2) S_2^2. \tag{5.18}$$

The derivative of the above with respect to w_1 is

$$\frac{dV_p}{dw_1} = 2w_1 S_1^2 - 2S_2^2 + 2w_1 S_2^2 = 0. \tag{5.19}$$

Consequently

$$w_1^* = \frac{S_2^2}{S_1^2 + S_2^2}. \qquad (5.20)$$

In this case, unlike the first, risk will generally be minimised by holding a diversified portfolio, as illustrated in Figure 5.4, from which it can be seen that the locus of all possible combinations of risk and expected return which the investor can acquire by combining the two assets is the curved line A_1PA_2. In this case, the risk level of the portfolio P – and of many of the possible portfolios – is less than that of the safest individual asset.

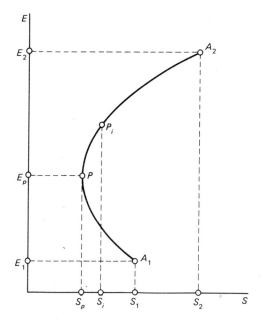

Figure 5.4

An important implication of this result is that even when the returns on the two assets are completely independent, it is still possible to reduce risk below that of the safest asset by holding a diversified portfolio. An inspection of Figure 5.4 will make it clear that all portfolios on the portfolio opportunity locus below the point P are dominated – that is to say, that for any risk level between S_p and

S_1, say S_i, there is a portfolio (P_i) on that part of the opportunity locus above P which dominates the portfolio at the same risk level below P. Thus none of the portfolios on the section below P would ever be chosen by a risk-averse investor.

Case Three: Perfect Negative Correlation

From the investor's point of view this is the most desirable situation of all. It occurs whenever the two assets are related and in such a way that a shortfall in the rate of return on the first asset below its mean is exactly offset by an increased return on the second asset above its mean. Perfect negative correlation implies that the covariance between the returns on the two assets is equal to the negative of the product of their standard deviations, i.e. $C_{12} = -S_1 S_2$. Consequently equation (5.5) may be rewritten as

$$V_p = w_1^2 S_1^2 + w_2^2 S_2^2 - 2w_1 w_2 S_1 S_2 \qquad (5.21)$$

$$= (w_1 S_1 - w_2 S_2)^2, \qquad (5.22)$$

so that

$$S_p = w_1 S_1 - w_2 S_2. \qquad (5.23)$$

The problem of finding the weights w_1^* and w_2^* which generate the minimum-risk portfolio is complicated in this instance by the fact that differential calculus cannot be employed since the locus of attainable risk–return combinations degenerates into two straight-line segments, as illustrated in Figure 5.5.

However, it may readily be demonstrated that S_p attains its lowest possible value of zero when w_1 is set equal to $S_2/(S_1 + S_2)$. It is left as an exercise for the reader to make this substitution in equation (5.22) and to verify that S_p does in fact attain the value of zero. In this example risk has been completely eliminated from the portfolio! This desirable state of affairs can only be achieved, however, when the two assets display perfect negative correlation. Needless to say, pairs of assets having this property are extremely rare in practice. The virtue in exploring this limiting case is that it highlights the principle that the existence of a high negative correlation between the assets is the source of risk reduction through diversification.

MULTI-ASSET PORTFOLIOS

The principle of risk reduction through diversification, which we have just examined in some detail for the two-asset case, may be

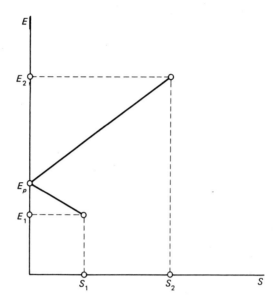

Figure 5.5

extended in a perfectly straightforward manner to portfolios consisting of three assets, four assets and, in general, N assets.

For example, if one already holds a two-asset portfolio having the characteristics E_p and V_p, and if one wishes to include a third asset having an expected rate of return E_3, the degree of risk reduction achieved by any given combination of the exiting portfolio and the third asset will depend on the extent of the covariance between the former and the latter, i.e. C_{p3}.

In general, in the N-asset case, let the weights $w_1, w_2, \ldots, w_N$ denote the proportions of initial wealth invested in each of the N assets. Then the expected rate of return on the portfolio is*

$$E_f = \sum_{i=1}^{N} w_i E_i, \qquad (5.24)$$

where E_i is the expected rate of return on the ith asset.

Denoting $w_1, w_2, \ldots, w_N$ by the column vector $\mathbf{w}^1$, and $E_1, E_2, \ldots, E_N$ by the column vector $\mathbf{e}$, equation (5.24) may be more succinctly expressed as

*See the Statistical Appendix, p. 137.

$$E_p = \mathbf{w}'\mathbf{e}, \tag{5.25}$$

where a prime denotes the transpose of a vector.

From equation (5.3) the variance of the portfolio may be expressed as

$$V_p = \sum_{i=1}^{N} \sum_{j=1}^{N} w_i w_j C_{ij}, \tag{5.26}$$

which may be similarly expressed in matrix notation as

$$V_p = \mathbf{w}'\mathbf{C}\mathbf{w}. \tag{5.27}$$

A specific choice of weights, the elements of the vector **w**, will thus imply a portfolio having a specific expected return, given by equation (5.25), and a specific variance, given by equation (5.27). Each element in **w** may vary from zero to unity – bearing in mind of course that they must sum to unity at all times, being proportions. Thus it follows that from any given set of N assets an infinite number of possible portfolios may be generated.

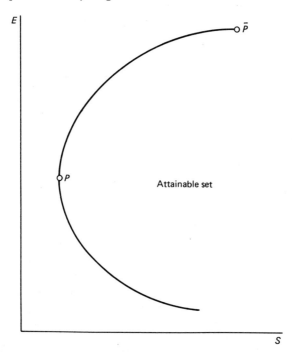

Figure 5.6

A point in *E–S* space (*E**, *S**) is said to be *attainable* if it is possible to select a portfolio from among those assets which constitute the asset universe having an expected return *E** and standard deviation *S**. The collection of all such portfolios is defined as the *attainable set*, or the *opportunity set*. A typical example of such an attainable set is illustrated in Figure 5.6.

The problem of portfolio selection may now be stated as that of choosing a vector of weights, **w**, which identifies that particular portfolio within the attainable set which best satisfies the investor's objectives – as expressed in his utility function.

As in the two-asset case, the majority of attainable portfolios will in practice be dominated by a relatively small sub-set, and so the problem of portfolio selection may be immediately reduced to that of choosing from among the set of undominated portfolios. Recalling the definition of dominance on page 68, it will be apparent that all undominated portfolios lie on that portion of the boundary of the attainable set denoted by $P\bar{P}$. This section of the boundary is known as the 'efficient frontier', or the 'efficient set'. Henceforth we need only concern ourselves with portfolios which lie on the efficient frontier.

The particular portfolio in the efficient set which best satisfies the investor's objectives is identified by superimposing his indifference map on Figure 5.6. This is illustrated in Figure 5.7, from which it may be seen that the investor reaches the highest attainable utility level – denoted in this case by the indifference curve labelled U_3 – by choosing the portfolio $\hat{P}$.

Other investors, having different degrees of risk-aversion, would have different-shaped indifference curves and would consequently choose portfolios other than $\hat{P}$.

With a large number of investors operating in the market it is reasonable to expect that many of the portfolios in the efficient set would in fact be held. But what becomes of those securities which do not enter any of the desired portfolios? Since nobody wishes to hold such securities, their prices will fall, thus, by implication, pushing up their expected rates of return – since their prospective yields are denominated in money terms – and making them more attractive to hold. For each such security, its attractiveness will continue to increase (because of the continuing decline in its price) until it reaches a point where some investor will find it desirable to include it in his optimal portfolio. The stronger the negative covariance between the security in question and the investor's currently-held portfolio, the less will be the necessary fall in the price of the security. Thus for the market as a whole all securities will be held and will form part of *some* efficient portfolio.

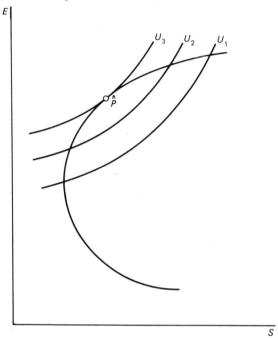

Figure 5.7

RISKLESS ASSETS AND LENDING PORTFOLIOS

The next stage in the analysis is to introduce a new type of asset into the asset universe in the form of a riskless bond. (A riskless bond is, by definition, devoid of default risk, capital risk and income risk, and so must mature at the end of the current time period.) The existence of such an asset has considerable implications for the theory of portfolio selection.

The riskless bond, L, may naturally be combined with any portfolio in the attainable set – and, more relevantly, on the efficient boundary – to form a new portfolio, the characteristics of which will depend on the ratio in which the two are combined. For example, let P_1 be a risky portfolio having the characteristics E_1 and S_1, and let the riskless bond L bear the certain rate of return r. Since the bond is riskless, both its own standard deviation of return S_L and the covariance between its return and that of P_1 are zero. The new port-folio, consisting of a combination of P_1 and L, with weights w_1 and $1 - w_1$ respectively, will have the characteristics implied by the straightforward application of equations (5.1) and (5.5) respectively, ie.

$$E_p = w_1 E_1 + (1 - w_1)r \qquad (5.28)$$

and

$$S_p = w_1 S_1. \qquad (5.29)$$

(To arrive at expression (5.29) we must bear in mind that, since V_2 and C_{12} are both zero, (5.5) reduces to

$$V_p = w_1^2 V_1,$$

and recall that $S_p = \sqrt{V_p}$ and that $w_1 S_1 = \sqrt{w_1^2 V_1}$.)

Dividing equation (5.29) through by S_1, we can express w_1 as

$$w_1 = \frac{S_p}{S_1}, \qquad (5.30)$$

and by substituting for w_1 in equation (5.28) from the above, and rearranging, we obtain

$$E_p = r + \frac{E_1 - r}{S_1} S_p, \qquad (5.31)$$

which is a linear equation in the variables E_p and S_p, having an intercept r and a slope $(E_1 - r)/S_1$. Thus the locus of all possible com-binations of P_1 and L is the straight line joining them – as illustrated in Figure 5.8.

Although the riskless bond L may be combined with any portfolio on the efficient boundary, the concept of dominance implies that there is typically one unique portfolio $\bar{P}$ which, when combined with L, will dominate all combinations with other risky portfolios below $\bar{P}$ on the efficient boundary. $\bar{P}$ is located at the point of tan-gency between the straight line originating from L and the efficient boundary.

The new efficient boundary is thus the line $L\bar{P}P$. There are now two types of portfolio which the investor may hold. Investors who have a relatively high degree of risk-aversion, such as investor A (depicted in Figure 5.8), will place part of their wealth in the optimal risky portfolio $\bar{P}$ and with the remainder of their wealth will purchase riskless bonds – i.e. lend it out at the rate of interest r. All such portfolios are referred to as 'lending portfolios'. Investors with a relative low degree of risk-aversion, such as investor B in the figure, will continue to hold high-risk, pure portfolios.

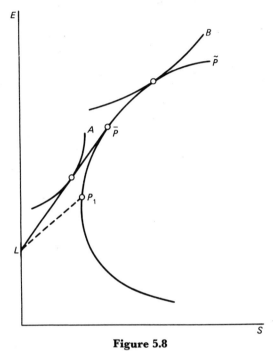

Figure 5.8

LEVERAGE AND BORROWING PORTFOLIOS

We consider next the case where the investor can lend money at the riskless rate of interest r and can *also* borrow funds at the same rate of interest. Here once again we are assuming the existence of a perfect capital market. The use of such borrowed funds to supplement one's own wealth for the purchase of a risk portfolio is termed 'leverage'. The basic effect of leverage is that it magnifies both the expected rate of return and the standard deviation of return on one's own wealth. The following numerical example illustrates how this arises.

Assume that an investor is offered shares in a risky venture which has only two possible outcomes. He will lose 10 per cent of his investment in the unfavourable case (which has a probability of occurrence of 0.25), or gain a 40 per cent profit on his outlay in the favourable case (which has a probability of occurrence of 0.75). Funds for borrowing are freely available up to a limit of £90,000 at an interest rate of 15 per cent per annum. The investor is prepared to consider investing £10,000 of his own wealth in the project, which would yield him an expected rate of return of 27.5 per cent with a standard deviation of 22 per cent. However, were he to borrow the £90,000 and invest it as well, the expected return on his own wealth would increase from 27.5 per cent to 240.0 per cent! However, this gain is not costless, for the risk on his investment (i.e. the standard deviation of the rate of return on his own wealth) would also increase *pari passu* from 21.7 per cent to 323.2 per cent. The arithmetic on which these conclusions are based is presented in Table 5.1, which is largely self-explanatory.

Table 5.1

		Case 1: unleveraged portfolio (£)	Case 2: leveraged portfolio (£)
(1)	Own wealth	10,000	10,000
(2)	Borrowed funds	0	90,000
(3)	Total amount invested (1 + 2)	10,000	100,000
(4)	Possible outcomes		
	(i) Lose 10 per cent (with probability 0.25)	9,000	90,000
	(ii) Gain 40 per cent (with probability 0.75)	14,000	140,000
(5)	Expected gross return	12,750	127,500
(6)	*Less* payment of interest and loan capital	0	103,500
(7)	Residual expected final wealth (5 − 6)	12,750	24,000
(8)	Expected rate of return on own wealth	27.5 per cent	240.0 per cent
(9)	Standard deviation of return on own wealth	21.7 per cent	323.2 per cent

The expected gross return (row 5) is calculated for the unleveraged case as follows:

$$£9000 \times 0.25 + £14,000 \times 0.75 = £12,750,$$

and analogously for the leveraged case. The interest component in row 6 for the leveraged case is £13,500, being 15 per cent of £90,000−

the project, for the sake of simplicity, being assumed to be of one year's duration.

The above example may readily be extended by assuming that the £90,000 is merely an upper limit – the investor may, if he so desires, borrow part of it.

The solution to this more general problem may readily be seen by referring to Figure 5.9. Three points in this figure are of particular interest. The point *L* represents the situation where the investor places all his wealth in the riskless asset (i.e. places it all in riskless bonds, as opposed to undertaking the risky venture). The point *P* represents the situation where he places all his wealth (£10,000) in the risky venture, and last the point *B* represents the situation where he places both his own wealth and the maximum amount he can borrow (£90,000) in the risky venture.

Just as the straight line joining the points *L* and *P* forms the locus of all portfolios in which part of the wealth is held in the risky asset and part in the riskless, so also the straight line joining the points *P* and *B* forms the locus of all portfolios which are leveraged by borrowed funds, ranging in amount from zero (at point *P*) to £90,000 (at point *B*). The line *BL* is aptly named the 'borrowing–lending line', and represents the range of all possible portfolios in which the investor can invest. The particular point (portfolio) which the investor chooses on the line depends, as always, on the shape of his indifference curves. The investor illustrated in Figure 5.9 chooses a portfolio $\bar{P}$, in which he has undertaken some leverage but not the maximum amount available.

Notice that no matter how low the investor's degree of risk-aversion, he can never go beyond the point *B*. In order to do so he would have to acquire additional borrowed funds. The length of the segment *PB* is determined by the amount of borrowed funds available.

PORTFOLIO SELECTION IN IMPERFECT CAPITAL MARKETS

The convenient assumption that borrowing and lending interest rates are the same may now be dropped as we explore the implications of the existence of an imperfect capital market on the theory of portfolio selection.

Two cases are of interest: first, the situation where the borrowing rate is constant for any amount borrowed but is higher than the lending rate; and second, the situation where the borrowing rate is not only higher than the lending rate but also increases as the amount borrowed gets larger. This latter case depicts a situation in which, as the primary source of capital dries up, the investor taps more expensive secondary sources.

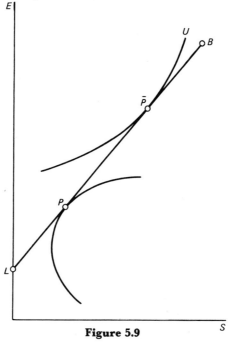

Figure 5.9

The implications of relaxing the assumption of a perfect capital market may best be illustrated diagrammatically, as in Figure 5.10. Let r_1 be the rate at which funds can be lent; then, by the arguments of the previous section, the straight line r_1P_1, originating from r_1 and tangent to the risky-asset efficient frontier, constitutes the relevant efficient boundary as far as P_1. Unfortunately for the investor he cannot continue along the dashed section of r_1A due to the imperfection of the capital market. If he wishes to leverage the portfolio P_1 he must borrow at an interest rate r_b – the borrowing rate. Thus his leveraged opportunity set is P_1C, which, since it lies inside the efficient boundary, is clearly sub-optimal. Given the borrowing rate r_b, the optimal portfolio to leverage is P_b, which gives him an opportunity set P_bB. This dominates all portfolios on the original efficient frontier to the right of P_b. However, all portfolios on the original efficient frontier between P_1 and P_b remain undominated. So for the investor in an imperfect capital market the complete efficient frontier is $r_1 P_1 P_b B$.

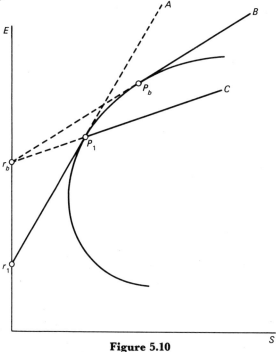

Figure 5.10

Consider next the implications of a decrease in the rate at which funds may be borrowed from r_{b1} to r_{b2}. This is illustrated in Figure 5.11, from which it may be seen that the optimal leveraged portfolio changes from P_{b1} to P_{b2}. Since the opportunity locus $P_{b2} A_2$ is at every point steeper than the original opportunity locus $P_{b2} P_{b1} A_1$, the investor is now being offered additional increments of risk at more attractive terms. The slope of the opportunity locus may thus be interpreted as the *price of risk* – it is the number of additional units of expected return that the investor receives in return for undertaking one additional unit of risk. Thus a change in the riskless interest rate will alter the price of risk, and so, since investors are assumed to have constant attitudes towards risk, affects the willingness of investors to hold risky assets.

Finally, let us consider the case in which the rate of interest at which funds may be borrowed increases as the sum borrowed increases. In order to analyse this case it is important to bear in mind that in previous examples no distinction was made – nor was one necessary – between the average rate of interest and the marginal rate (or the rate on the last pound borrowed). Since the rate of interest was constant, the two concepts coincided. However, such a distinction must be maintained in the present case. By the term 'the cost of borrowed funds' we shall mean the average interest rate paid for a borrowed sum of a given size. The essence of this case is that the cost of borrowed funds increases with the size of the sum borrowed.

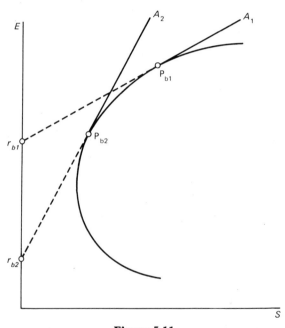

Figure 5.11

It may be seen from Figure 5.11 that an increase in the cost of borrowing leads to an increase in the riskiness of the optimal leveraged portfolio. That relationship provides the basis for the analysis of the present case, the solution to which may be seen in Figure 5.12.

Let r_1 be the lowest borrowing rate obtainable, and let us assume that the maximum amount which can be borrowed at that rate will allow a leveraged portfolio up to the point B_1. Thus r_1B_1 forms the first part of the borrowing–lending line. If the investor wishes to leverage his portfolio beyond B_1, the additional funds borrowed will be at a higher interest rate r_1', thus raising the average cost of borrowing and changing the optimal portfolio to be leveraged. Eventually, when the maximum sum available at interest rate r_1' has been borrowed, the average cost of borrowing will have increased to, say, r_2 and the maximum leverage obtainable will be, say, B_2. As the amount borrowed at r_1' increases from zero to the maximum sum available, a continuous path will be traced out from B_1 to B_2, represented by the dotted line in Figure 5.12. Each point on this path, for example B_j, represents the maximum leveraged portfolio obtainable at the particular interest rate r_j. Since r_j is continually changing, due to the fact that the marginal cost of borrowing is above the average, the only undominated portfolio, leveraged from r_j, is the portfolio at the end-point of the borrowing–lending line, r_jB_j, namely the portfolio B_j. This may be seen more clearly from Figure 5.12.

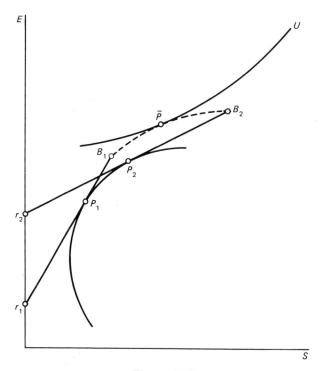

Figure 5.12

The path B_1B_2 thus forms the remaining segment of the efficient locus (by definition), and given the shape of his indifference curves the investor will choose some portfolio such as $\bar{P}$ on the locus $r_1B_1B_2$.

Should additional funds become available at an interest rate higher than r_1', it is a straightforward matter to repeat the above procedure and extend the efficient locus beyond B_2.

CHAPTER 6

Index Models for Portfolio Selection

The amount of time and information required to generate an efficient portfolio increases at an alarming rate as the number of securities in the asset universe approaches a realistic magnitude. If the number of securities in the asset universe is n, then, before any portfolio selection can be undertaken, it is first of all necessary to calculate n expected rates of return and $(n^2 + n)/2$ variances and covariances. Table 6.1 gives some indication of the order of magnitude of the necessary input requirements and of the consequent limitations which are imposed on the practical implementation of the Markowitz framework described in Chapter 5.

Table 6.1

Number of Securities	10	50	100	500	1000
Number of inputs required	65	1325	5150	125,750	501,500

Not surprisingly, considerable effort has been devoted to the problem of finding ways of cutting down on the input requirements such that the mean–variance framework for portfolio selection may be applied at reasonable cost to large security universes. In the following sections we examine two closely related approaches to this problem – Sharpe's *single-index* or *diagonal* model, and its extension, the *multi-index* model.

The Single-index Model

Index models owe their origin to a seminal paper by Sharpe which introduced a simple but far-reaching modification to the basic

Markowitz framework.[1] Sharpe added an additional assumption that the observed covariance between the returns on individual securities is attributable to the common dependence of security yields upon a single common external force – a market index.*

The major characteristic of the diagonal model is the assumption that the returns of various securities are related only through common relationship with some basic underlying factor. The return from any security is determined solely by random factors and this single outside element; more explicitly

$$r_i = a_i + b_i I + u_i \tag{6.1}$$

which states that the return on the ith security, r_i, depends linearly upon the current value of a relevant market index, I, where a_i and b_i are parameters (or constants) which specify the exact nature of the relationship, and u_i is a random disturbance which has a mean of zero and a finite variance – var$[u_i]$. Such a relationship is depicted in Figure 6.1.

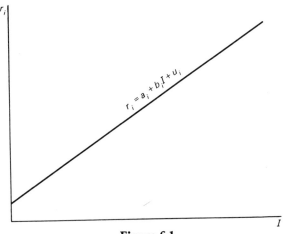

Figure 6.1

An essential feature of this specification is that the residual random disturbances between any pair of securities are uncorrelated with each other – that is to say, cov$[u_i, u_j] = 0$, for all i and j such that $i \neq j$.

*Sharpe's notation has been altered slightly in order to make it compatible with that of the rest of this book.

The index I is assumed, in the single-index model, to be the sole non-random factor affecting the yield on each security in the asset universe. Its future value is not predetermined and so is not known with certainty. However, one may refer meaningfully to the expected value of the index – $E[I]$ – and to the uncertainty as to its future value, as measured by its variance – $\text{var}[I]$.

One last specification of this model is that the probability distribution of the index is independent of the probability distribution of the disturbance u_i in equation (6.1). More specifically, it is assumed that $\text{cov}[I,u_i] = 0$ for all i, which is to say that the covariance between the index I and the random disturbance u_i is zero for every value of $_i$.

In view of the above specification of the model it is a straightforward matter to derive the following relationships:

(1) The expected return on the ith security is (by taking expectations in equation (6.1))

$$E[r_i] = a_i + b_i E[I]. \qquad (6.2)$$

Thus if the values of a_i, b_i and $E[I]$ are known, it is possible to estimate $E[r_i]$.

If we let w_i denote the proportion of total wealth held in the form of the ith asset, then the total portfolio may be denoted by the vector $w' = (w_1, w_2, \ldots, w_n)$, and the actual rate of return on the portfolio is given by r_p, where r_p is defined as $\sum\limits_{i=1}^{n} w_i r_i$, which, on substituting for r_i from equation (6.1), becomes

$$\begin{aligned} r_p = w_1 a_1 + w_2 a_2 + \ldots + w_n a_n + \\ [w_1 b_1 + w_2 b_2 + \ldots + w_n b_n] I + \\ w_1 u_1 + w_2 u_2 + \ldots + w_n u_n. \end{aligned} \qquad (6.3)$$

Denoting the bracketed expression (6.3) as b_I, the expected return on the portfolio may be written as

$$E[r_p] = w_1 a_1 + w_2 a_2 + \ldots + w_n a_n + b_I E[I], \qquad (6.4)$$

since the expected value of each random variable $u_1, \ldots, u_n$ is zero. by assumption, and consequently the expected value of any weighted sum $\sum\limits_{i=1}^{n} w_i u_i$ is also zero.

(2) Next, recalling the assumption that the covariance between

the index I and each of the random disturbances u_i is zero, and that the covariance between any u_i and u_j $(j \neq i)$ is also zero, the variance of return on the portfolio may be written as*

$$\text{var}[r_p] = w_1^2\text{var}[u_1] + w_2^2\text{var}[u_2] + \ldots + w_n^2\text{var}[u_n] + b_1^2\text{var}[I]. \tag{6.5}$$

Since the above expressions are beginning to become somewhat unwieldly when written in scaler notation, it will be convenient to restate them in matrix notation as follows. Let

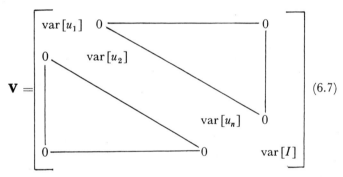

$$\mathbf{z} = \begin{bmatrix} w_1 \\ \cdot \\ \cdot \\ \cdot \\ w_n \\ b_I \end{bmatrix} \quad \mathbf{a} = \begin{bmatrix} a_1 \\ \cdot \\ \cdot \\ \cdot \\ a_n \\ E[I] \end{bmatrix} \tag{6.6}$$

and

$$\mathbf{V} = \begin{bmatrix} \text{var}[u_1] & 0 & & & 0 \\ 0 & \text{var}[u_2] & & & \\ & & \ddots & & \\ & & & \text{var}[u_n] & 0 \\ 0 & & & 0 & \text{var}[I] \end{bmatrix} \tag{6.7}$$

Thus expression (6.4) becomes

$$E[r_p] = \mathbf{a}'\mathbf{z}, \tag{6.8}$$

where the primed vector denotes a row vector; and expression (6.5) becomes

$$\text{var}[r_p] = \mathbf{z}'\mathbf{V}\mathbf{z}. \tag{6.9}$$

Since the rationale for constructing the index model is to economise on the number of necessary data inputs, it is worth while examining expressions (6.4) and (6.5) (or, equivalently, (6.8) and (6.9)) in

---

*See the Statistical Appendix, p. 137, for the formula for the variance of a sum of uncorrelated random variables.

order to see the extent to which this objective has been achieved.

The input requirements now consist of the $n + 1$ elements of the vector $\mathbf{a}$ and the $n + 1$ diagonal elements of the matrix $\mathbf{V}$ (since, by assumption, the off-diagonal elements of $\mathbf{V}$ are zero). Altogether this amounts to $2n + 2$ input requirements, as opposed to $(n^2 + n)/2$ for the full Markowitz model. The saving in the volume of input data is thus considerable and becomes increasingly important as the number of securities in the asset universe increases. The comparison of the input requirements for the two models is shown graphically in Figure 6.2.

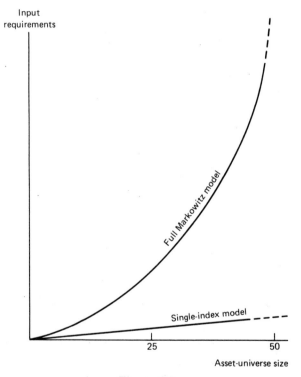

Figure 6.2

SYSTEMATIC AND UNSYSTEMATIC ASSET RISK

Recalling that the basic relationship underpinning Sharpe's single-index model is

$$r_i = a_i + b_i I + u_i, \qquad i = 1, \ldots, n, \tag{6.10}$$

it may be seen that the variability in the rate of return on the ith security can be attributed to two sources: first, the random disturbance u_i affects r_i in each time period contributing to the uncertainty as to the latter's value; second, the future value of the market index is not known in advance with certainty, and variations in it will also affect r_i – as indeed it will affect every asset in the asset universe to a greater or lesser extent – since all assets are functions of the index I. The greater the absolute value of b_i, the more responsive will be the value of r_i to changes in the market index I.

The breakdown in the variability in r_i into its component parts may best be seen as follows:

$$\text{var}\,[r_i] = E[r_i - E[r_i]]^2 \tag{6.11}$$

$$= E[((a_i + b_iI + u_i) - E[a_i + b_iI + u_i]]^2, \tag{6.12}$$

which, on multiplying out, becomes

$$\text{var}\,[r_i] = E[a_i + b_iI + u_i - E[a_i] - b_iE[I] - E[u_i]]^2, \tag{6.13}$$

which, since a_i is a constant giving $E[a_i] = a_i$, gives, on rearranging

$$\text{var}\,[r_i] = E[b_i\{I - E[I]\} + [u_i - E[u_i]]^2 \tag{6.14}$$

$$= b_1^2 E[I - E[I]]^2 + E[u_i]^2 \tag{6.15}$$

$$= b_1^2 \text{var}\,[I] + \text{var}\,[u_i] \tag{6.16}$$

$$= \text{systematic risk} + \text{unsystematic risk}.$$

The two components into which the variance of r_i has been decomposed are clearly identified in equation (6.16). The first component was given the title systematic risk by Sharpe, since its source is the variance of the market index I. It is systematic in the sense that the market index affects all securities in the asset universe to a greater or lesser extent (depending on the absolute value of the coefficient b_i).

The second term – 'unsystematic risk' – derives from the random disturbance u_i, which is, of course, specific to the ith asset. Var$[u_i]$ may appropriately be interpreted as the variance of r_i conditional upon a given value of the market index I:

$$\text{var}\,[u_i] = \text{var}\,[r_i|I]. \tag{6.17}$$

where the vertical stroke on the right-hand side means 'conditional upon'. Unsystematic risk is, in other words, that variation in r_i which is still unaccounted for after the variation in the market index I has been eliminated. Lintner refers to the unsystematic risk as the *residual variance*.[2]

SYSTEMATIC RISK AND RISK REDUCTION THROUGH
NAÏVE DIVERSIFICATION

The term 'naïve diversification' is used to describe the type of portfolio which consists of a collection of randomly chosen assets. It would seem reasonable to expect that as the number of assets included in a portfolio increases, the variance of return on the portfolio should decrease – due to the cancelling-out of individual fluctuations in asset yields. Such intuition would be well-founded and forms the rationale behind naïvely diversified portfolios.

However, it is not possible to reduce risk to zero simply by increasing the number of assets held in the portfolio. There exists a lower limit below which risk cannot be reduced through naïve diversification, no matter how many assets are included in the portfolio. This lower limit is, as we shall see, the level of systematic risk.

Consider a portfolio consisting of equal cash purchases of K different securities. The risk measure of such a portfolio is, by equation (6.5),

$$\text{var}[r_p] = \frac{1}{K^2}\text{var}[u_1] + \ldots + \frac{1}{K^2}\text{var}[u_K] + b_I^2\text{var}[I], \quad (6.18)$$

since $w_i = 1/K$, given that an equal amount of wealth is invested in each of the K securities (total wealth being 'normalised' to unity). By rearranging the terms, equation (6.18) may readily be rewritten as

$$\text{var}[r_p] = \frac{1}{K}\left\{\frac{\text{var}[u_1] + \ldots + \text{var}[u_K]}{K}\right\} + b_I^2\text{var}[I], \quad (6.19)$$

where the term inside the braces is a measure of the average residual variance of the securities in the portfolio. It is clear from equation (6.19) that as the number of assets in the portfolio (K) is increased, the relatively constant term within the braces is multiplied by a diminishing fraction $1/K$. Consequently, in the limit, as K gets indefinitely large, the first term on the right-hand side of equation (6.19) tends to zero, and so var $[r_p]$ tends to its lower limit of $b_I^2\text{var}[I]$, which is of course the measure of systematic risk in equation (6.16).

What is perhaps surprising is the speed with which the risk of a portfolio approaches the asymptotic lower level of systematic risk. Evans and Archer,[3] in a study of random portfolios constructed from securities quoted on the New York stock exchange, produced empirical evidence which implies that a relatively low level of diversification – say eight or nine different securities – can eliminate most of the non-systematic risk from a portfolio. Their results are ll ustrated graphically in Figure 6.3.

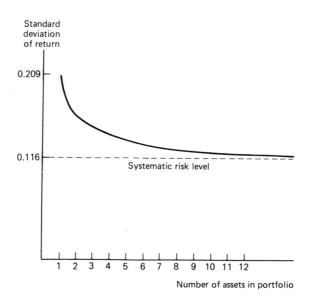

Figure 6.3 *Risk reduction through naïve diversification*

NAÏVE VERSUS MARKOWITZ DIVERSIFICATION

It is important to maintain a clear distinction between the type of diversification which has just been discussed – naïve diversification – and the type of diversification which was discussed in the previous section – Markowitz diversification.

It is important to note that the rationale behind the two activities is completely different. In the case of naïve diversification the objective is to reduce risk, by increasing the number of assets held, to the market average of risk (i.e. systematic risk). This activity relies on the principle that the non-systematic component of the level of risk tends to disappear as K (the number of assets held) increases.

Naïve diversification can never (except by chance) reduce risk below the market average level.

Markowitz diversification, on the other hand, does not rely on large asset numbers to reduce risk, but instead searches for assets which have relatively strong negative covariance with one another. In extreme cases it is (at least theoretically) possible that risk could be completely eliminated with a portfolio consisting of only two (perfectly negatively correlated) assets, as illustrated in Figure 6.4. It follows that Markowitz diversification *can* reduce risk below the market average. The corollary is that, as more and more securities are forced into a Markowitz-diversified portfolio, its risk level will rise towards the market average, as illustrated in Figure 6.4, due to the erosion of the gains from Markowitz diversification by the inclusion of positively correlated securities.

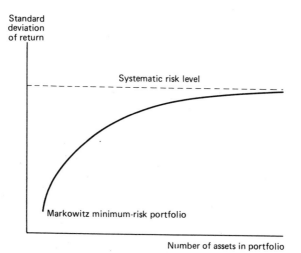

Figure 6.4 *Effects of Markowitz diversification*

Multi-index Models

The price to be paid for obtaining the savings in input requirements of the single-index model is the acceptance of what may be seen as the somewhat restrictive assumptions of that model – namely that there exists a single index which constitutes the sole non-random influence on all of the securities in the security universe.

If the assets are all of a similar nature – e.g. all property shares – the above assumption may not be unduly restrictive; but if they are assets with widely disparate characteristics, then one may be tempted to hesitate before accepting the single-index framework.

However, a compromise is possible, and it lies in the extension of the index principle from a single index to several such indices. Suppose that the rate of return on the ith asset is jointly determined by several factors (represented by indices) and that the relationship may be summarised in the following equation:

$$r_i = a_i + b_{i1}I_1 + b_{i2}I_2 + \ldots + b_{im}I_m + u_i, \qquad (6.20)$$

where $I_1, I_2, \ldots, I_m$ are the values of the m separate indices, and u_i is, as before, a random disturbance term with zero mean and a known variance, $\mathrm{var}[u_i]$; the coefficients $b_{i1}, b_{i2}, \ldots, b_{im}$ measure the responsiveness of r_i to changes in each of the indices in turn.

The sole non-random factors affecting the rates of return of all assets in the universe are assumed, in multi-index models, to be the m indices, though the impact of any individual index may vary from one asset to another; that is to say, there is no reason why b_{i1} should be the same as b_{j1} since the first index might heavily affect the return on the ith asset but have a small or negligible impact on the jth asset. Similarly, there is no reason why some of the bs should not be zero in the equation for a given asset – which would imply that the corresponding index had no effect on the rate of return of that asset.

From equation (6.20) the expected rate of return on the ith asset is readily derived as

$$E[r_i] = a_i + b_{i1}E[I_1] + \ldots + b_{im}E[I_m], \qquad (6.21)$$

since a_i is a constant and $E[u_i]$ is zero, by assumption.

As in the single-index case, we may express the rate of return on any given portfolio $w = (w_1, w_2, \ldots, w_n)$ as a linear combination of the rates of return on its component assets as follows:

$$
\begin{aligned}
r_p = {}& w_1 a_1 + \ldots + w_n a_n \\
& + w_1 b_{11} I_1 + \ldots + w_n b_{n1} I_1 \\
& \qquad \vdots \\
& + w_1 b_{1m} I_m + \ldots + w_n b_{nm} I_m \\
& + w_1 u_1 + \ldots + w_n u_n.
\end{aligned}
\qquad (6.22)
$$

Letting

$$b_{pi}I_i = (w_1 b_{1i} + \ldots w_n b_{ni})I_i, \qquad (6.23)$$

equation (6.22) may be simplified to read

$$r_p = \sum_{i=1}^{n} w_i a_i + \sum_{i=1}^{n} b_{pi}I_i + \sum_{i=1}^{n} w_i u_i, \qquad (6.24)$$

and, to derive the expression for the expected rate of return on the portfolio, we take the expectation of equation (6.24) to obtain

$$E[r_p] = \sum_{i=1}^{n} w_i a_i + \sum_{i=1}^{n} b_{pi} E[I_i], \qquad (6.25)$$

since $\sum_{i=1}^{n} w_i E[u_i] = 0$, by assumption.

In order to derive the expression for the standard deviation of the multi-index portfolio, we need to specify our assumptions more explicitly. From equation (6.24) it may be seen that the variance of return on the portfolio may be expressed as the variance of a sum of random variables:

$$\text{var}[r_p] = \text{var}\left[\sum_{i=1}^{n} b_{pi}I_i + \sum_{i=1}^{n} w_i u_i \right]. \qquad (6.26)$$

In order to evaluate the above expression it is necessary to know what assumptions are made about the covariances between the various terms in the sum. Specifically:

  (i) Is the covariance between every pair of disturbance terms, u_i and u_j, equal to zero?
  (ii) Is the covariance between every index and every disturbance term I_i and u_j equal to zero?
  (iii) Is the covariance between every pair of indices, I_i and I_j, equal to zero?

If the answer to (i), (ii) and (iii) is 'yes', the the variance of the rate of return on the portfolio may be expressed as*

$$\text{var}[r_p] = \sum_{i=1}^{n} b_{pi}^2 \text{var}[I_i] + \sum_{i=1}^{n} w_i^2 \text{var}[u_i]. \qquad (6.27)$$

Just how likely is it that (i), (ii) and (iii) can, in practice, be

---

*See the Statistical Appendix, p. 137, for the formula for the variance of a sum of random variables.

answered in the affirmative? As far as condition (i) is concerned, it is highly probable that u_i and u_j will not be correlated – provided that one has been essentially correct in one's choice of the relevant indices. Indeed, a non-zero covariance between u_i and u_j might legitimately be interpreted as an indication that the index model had been mis-specified, in that some index, which had not been included, was systematically disturbing both the ith and jth equation simultaneously.

Similarly, condition (ii) is likely to be met in practice. It is, moreover, a commonly held assumption in regression models of this type.

Condition (iii), however, is somewhat more tenuous. There is no compelling reason why the indices should not be correlated with one another. In fact the likelihood is that the types of variables that one would wish to include as indices would be highly correlated with one another.

All is not lost, however. There are two routes out of this dilemma. The first is to combine the m basic indices together so as to produce m new indices which will not be correlated with one another.[4]

The second approach is to compute the covariances among the indices and express the portfolio variance – according to formula (A.13) on page 137 – as

$$\text{var}[r_p] = \sum_{i=1}^{m} b_i^2 \text{var}[u_i] + \sum_{i=1}^{m} \sum_{j=1}^{m} b_i b_j \text{cov}[I_i, I_j]. \quad (6.28)$$

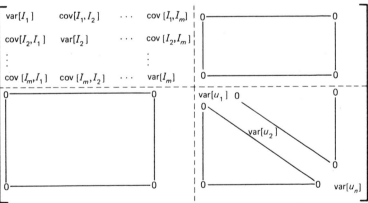

Figure 6.5 *Covariance matrix for multi-index model*

Strictly speaking the model is no longer a diagonal model but rather a block-diagonal model, as the covariance matrix (which constitutes a major component of the required data input) now looks like Figure 6.5.

Thus the penalty which must be paid for using correlated indices is that the full covariance matrix must be estimated for the m indices; this is of dimension $m \times m$. Clearly, as the number of indices, m, approaches the number of securities in the asset universe, n, the potential gains in input reduction from using the diagonal model becomes limited.

In index models, then, the trade-off lies between the number of inputs which must be estimated and the number of simplifying assumptions one is willing to make.

CHAPTER 7

The Efficiency of Security Markets

Characteristics of an Efficient Market

The market conditions under which a good can be traded are of many types and have in the past been diligently classified by economists. There may be just a single seller – a monopolist – or there may be several sellers acting in unison – collusive oligopolists. Alternatively, they may not collude, or their numbers may be so great as to preclude a stable collusion. Similarly, on the demand side there may be just a single purchaser or a small group of purchasers, colluding or otherwise, or a large number of purchasers.

The various permutations of supply and demand conditions give rise to various models of markets, and it is with one such model that we are concerned here – that of an *efficient market*. The following is an account of the conditions which prevail in an efficient market.

First, it is assumed that a large number of both buyers and sellers operate freely without transactions costs, in the trading of a homogeneous commodity. The market is assumed to be an active one, in that a substantial volume of trading is taking place all the time. Furthermore, the commodity being traded is assumed to have an infinite life span and so may be brought back to the market and retraded at any time. It is also capable of being stored costlessly for an indefinite period of time. Last, and most important, a 'sufficient number' of traders are assumed to have instant access to all available information which would affect the value of the commodity being traded. By 'sufficient number' is meant a number large enough to render collusion unviable.

The essential characteristic of an efficient market is that at every instant in time the price at which the commodity is traded accurately represents the traders' assessment of its value. Contrast this with, say, an auction at which only two members of the audience are art experts and who form a pact not to bid against one another for a valuable work of art. In this latter case the price at which the object is sold is *not* an accurate reflection of the traders' (which term includes the two art experts) assessment of its value. Such a situation is not possible in an efficient market due to the instantaneous information flows which exist in it.

One interesting and very important phenomenon which is to be observed in an efficient market is that all price changes which occur are of a random nature; that is to say, there are no systematic patterns to be observed over time in the price of the commodity. It is straightforward to establish that this feature follows directly from the nature of the market. Consider the advent of a new piece of information which will favourably affect the intrinsic value of the commodity. One possible manifestation of systematic price movement would be a steady increase in the price of the commodity as in Figure 7.1, over a period of time during which more and more traders received and acted upon this information.

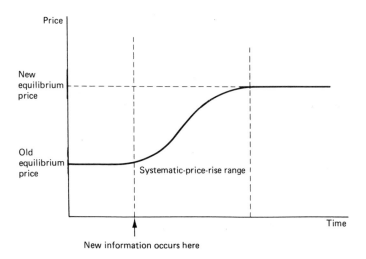

Figure 7.1

In an efficient market, however, such a price pattern would not occur, this for two reasons. First, if the traders who received the information initially had sufficient resources, it would be in their interest to push the price up to its new equilibrium level immediately – by purchasing the commodity in sufficient quantity. As long as it is being traded at a price which is below its equilibrium, there is clearly a profit to be made by purchasing it with a view to later resale.

However, if these traders did not have sufficient resources to do this, they would nevertheless have a valuable asset in the information they possess and it would be in their interest to sell this information immediately to other traders who did have the necessary resources. Either way, it is safe to conclude that the response of the market price to the new information would be virtually instantaneous.

The only other potential sources of systematic price patterns is where a commodity tends to exhibit regular periodic price movements, as in Figure 7.2. This is the sort of price pattern that one might possibly expect to observe in, for example, the market for foreign exchange, where, at regular intervals, large payments have to be made in foreign currency.

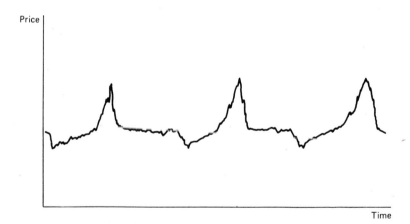

Figure 7.2 *Systematic price movements*

In an efficient market, however, the simple process of arbitrage would immediately eliminate such a non-random pattern as soon as it was recognised as such, leaving as before only the residual random price movements.

The concept of an efficient market is clearly nothing more than a theoretical artefact, so why should one be interested in its characteristics? The answer to this question has to do with an important characteristic of efficient markets, namely that, in such a market, today's price conveys no information to the traders as to what the price will be tomorrow – since price changes are completely random. It is thus impossible for a trader in an efficient market to outwit the other traders by gleaning information about future prices from present or past price movements.

There currently exists a heated controversy between two opposing schools as to whether or not security markets behave as if they were efficient markets. Those who believe that security markets are efficient are proponents of the *random-walk hypothesis*, the nature of which we explore in the next section. They contend that in such markets successive price changes are independent random variables, and consequently that past price changes convey no information about future price changes. The other school, known as the *chartists*, deny the efficient character of security markets and maintain that they can, by means of various charts, predict the direction of future price changes by observing the pattern of past changes. If this claim is true, the chartists can of course generate profit for investors by making successful predictions. In the following sections we examine the relative merits of the two schools.

The Random-walk Hypothesis

This hypothesis addresses itself to a single issue, namely, whether from a statistical analysis of the past history of a stock's price movements it is possible to gain any information about the direction of future price movements. Stated formally, the random-walk hypothesis asserts that *successive security* price changes are independent random variables*.

Some additional definitions will be useful at this stage. Consider the following time sequence of stock prices beginning at an arbitrary initial date, which we can denote by the subscript zero, and ending at the present time, denoted by the subscript t:

$$P_0, P_1, P_2, \ldots, P_{t-1}, P_t, \qquad (7.1)$$

and suppose that at the present time, t, we wish to make a statement about the expected value of P_{t+1} in the light of all the information

---

*The hypothesis is also commonly applied to commodity prices, such as cocoa, copper, wheat, etc.

contained in the past history of the sequence. It is convenient to use
the expression

$$E[P_{t+1}|P_t, P_{t-1}, \ldots, P_0)$$ (7.2)

to denote this conditional expectation. Equivalently, we might write

$$E[P_{t+1}|P_{t-s}, \qquad s = 0, 1, 2, \ldots].$$ (7.3)

A sequence such as expression (7.1) is said to form a 'martingale'
if it has the following property:

$$E[P_{t+1}|P_t, P_{t-1}, \ldots, P_0] = P_t,$$ (7.4)

which is to say that the best prediction for next period's outcome, in
the light of the past history of the sequence, is the current value of the
sequence. The random-walk hypothesis is thus equivalent to the
hypothesis that the sequence of security prices forms a 'martingale'.

Expression (7.4) is consistent with the stock-price-generating
mechanism

$$P_{t+1} = P_t + e_t,$$ (7.5)

where e_t is a random disturbance having a zero mean, a constant
variance which, if unknown, may be estimated consistently from the
history of the sequence, and – most important – successive drawings
of the disturbance are statistically independent so that the covariance
between e_t and e_{t-s} is zero for all non-zero values of s. The above
properties of the disturbance may be stated formally as

$$\left.\begin{array}{ll} E[e_t] & = 0 \\ \mathrm{var}[e_t] & = k \text{ (a constant)} \\ \mathrm{cov}[e_t, e_{t-s}] & = 0 \text{ for all non-zero} \\ & \qquad \text{values of } s \end{array}\right\} \text{ for all } t$$ (7.6)

Alternatively, equation (7.5) may be expressed as

$$\Delta P_t = e_t,$$ (7.7)

where ΔP_t (pronounced 'delta P_t') is defined as $P_t - P_{t-1}$. From
equation (7.7) is is clear that the random-walk hypothesis asserts that
successive price changes behave as independent random variables
having a zero mean and a constant finite variance.

The hypothesis thus asserts that a stock's price history contains no
information concerning the direction of future price movements.

One fairly obvious weakness in the random-walk hypothesis arises from the fact that security prices are restricted by definition to be non-negative whereas the price-generating mechanism depicted in equation (7.7) contains nothing to prevent the occurrence of negative prices. This consideration has led to a variant to the basic random-walk hypothesis in which the logarithm of the price sequence is assumed to obey the random walk:

$$\log P_{t+1} = \log P_t + v_t. \tag{7.8}$$

The relationship between this formulation and the original one may be seen by dividing equation (7.5) on both sides by P_t to obtain

$$\frac{P_{t+1}}{P_t} = 1 + \frac{e_t}{P_t}. \tag{7.9}$$

Next, define $1 + e_t/P_t$ as u_t, which is of course a random variable, the expected value of which is unity provided that $E[e_t] = 0$. Taking logs of equation (7.9) we obtain

$$\log P_{t+1} = \log P_t + v_t, \tag{7.10}$$

where v_t is defined as $\log u_t$.

Where the percentage change in prices is fairly small, the two formulations of the random-walk hypothesis, equations (7.5) and (7.10), are approximately equivalent.

It is important to realise the limitations of the random-walk hypothesis. It is sometimes erroneously inferred that if prices obey a random walk then future price changes cannot be predicted. However, the random-walk hypothesis does not assert this. What it does assert is that one cannot make any such predictions on the basis of looking at past prices alone. It is perfectly consistent with the random-walk hypothesis that an astute security analyst could, on the basis of his view of the state of the economy and/or some similar indicators, make reliable predictions about the direction of future security price changes. It is the possibility of a very specific type of prediction which the random-walk hypothesis denies, namely a prediction based solely on an examination of past prices.

EMPIRICAL EVIDENCE ON THE RANDOM-WALK HYPOTHESIS

A substantial volume of work has taken place in recent years devising tests which would either substantiate or refute the random-walk hypothesis, and a brief summary of the results of these tests is given in this section.

The reader, accustomed to seeing in the newspapers such phrases as 'a rising market' or 'the stock market boom of the early 1970s' may at first find it odd that one should question the very existence of stock price trends. Yet the random-walk hypothesis does just that. It asserts that such observed 'trends' and 'patterns' are merely optical illusions produced by concentrating on price *levels* rather than on price *changes*.

In order to evaluate this argument, consider Figure 7.3. An eight-year sequence of successive monthly observations on the level of the *Financial Times* 500 shares index was taken. Successive price changes were noted and their distribution plotted. Random drawings were taken from this distribution and used to generate a new sequence (a genuine random walk). The original *Financial Times* index and the random sequence are compared in Figure 7.3. The reader is invited to compare 7.3(i) and 7.3(ii) and to decide which of the two is the original index and which the random sequence.

(i)

Figure 7.3 (i)

Figure 7.3 (ii)

The majority of tests of the random-walk hypothesis fall into three main categories – correlation tests, runs tests and filter tests – and we shall briefly examine each in turn.

Correlation Tests

If successive price changes are statistically independent random variables, then it follows, by definition, that the correlation between a price change and the immediately preceding price change is zero. This statistic is referred to as the 'first-order autocorrelation co-efficient' of the sequence. Thus if the points ΔP_t, ΔP_{t+1} $(t = 1, 2, \ldots)$ are plotted on a graph, the random-walk hypothesis implies that the scatter of points should look like Figure 7.4(iii), not like Figure 7.4(i) or Figure 7.4(ii). A scatter such as that in Figure 7.4(i) indicates a positive correlation, which implies that successive price changes tend to be in the same direction. This would produce trends in the graph of a stock's price level. A less apparent, though not less sig-nificant, form of non-randomness is illustrated in Figure 7.4(ii). Here successive price changes, because of the existence of negative correlation, would tend to be in opposite directions, thus producing a 'saw-tooth' effect in the graph of the stock's price level.

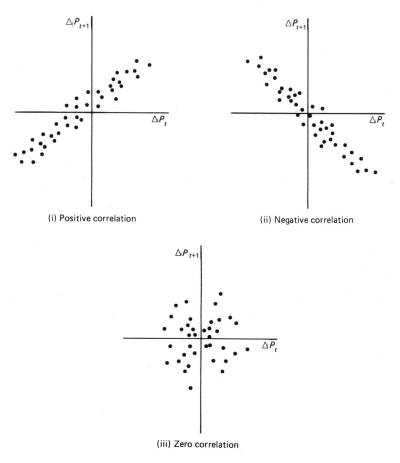

Figure 7.4

However, in addition to the above first-order effects, the statistical independence of successive price changes also implies that the correlation between a price change and the one which occurred two periods previously – the second-order autocorrelation – is also zero. In fact statistical independence implies, by definition, that the auto-correlation coefficients of every order are zero. This suggests a straightforward statistical test of the independence of the sequence of price changes – namely to compute the sample autocorrelations of the sequence and to ascertain whether they differ significantly from the expected value of zero.

Fama carried out such an experiment in which the autocorrelations of all orders from first to tenth were calculated on the proportionate price changes over a sample consisting of the thirty Dow Jones stocks.[1] The sample consisted of daily observations on the price of each stock over a five-year period, and the resulting calculated autocorrelation coefficients can be seen in Table 7.1.

In no case does the estimated coefficient differ significantly from zero. Thus the experiment lends strong support to the random-walk hypothesis. The Fama experiment is but one of a large number of similar experiments which have been undertaken with a view to identifying any possible evidence of autocorrelation in stock and commodity price movements.[2] Although the experiments in this field refer to widely different securities and time periods, the results are all broadly similar – no substantial evidence to suggest the existence of autocorrelation in stock price movements. The random-walk hypothesis would appear, then, to gain substantial credibility in the wake of the failure of successive experiments to find evidence of autocorrelation in stock price movements.

Runs Tests

An alternative way to test for randomness in a stock's price movements is to use a runs test. In this type of test the price movements are classified as being either positive $(+)$ or negative $(-)$, the size of the price change being ignored. Any sequence of price movements may then be characterised in the following manner:

$$+ + - + - - - + + - + - - - - - + + + - + +\qquad(7.11)$$

A run is defined as a sequence of the same sign. Thus in the sequence of price changes depicted in expression (7.11) above, there are eleven runs, identified as follows:

$$\underset{1}{+} \underset{2}{+} \underset{3}{-} \underset{4}{+} \underset{5}{- - -} \underset{6}{+} \underset{7}{+} \underset{8}{- + - - - -} \underset{9}{+ + +} \underset{10}{-} \underset{11}{+ +}\qquad(7.12)$$

Taking an independent random variable, it is possible, for a sample of any given size, to derive the expected number of runs. If, for example, you tossed a coin twenty times and, denoting a head by $(+)$ and a tail by $(-)$, you obtained the following sequence

Table 7.1

Estimated autocorrelation coefficients for thirty major stocks

Stocks	Lag (days)									
	1	2	3	4	5	6	7	8	9	10
Allied Chemicals	.02	−.04	.01	−.00	.03	.00	.02	−.03	−.02	−.01
Aluminium Co. of America	.12	.04	.01	.02	−.02	.01	.02	.01	−.00	−.03
American Can Co.	−.09	−.02	.03	−.07	−.02	−.01	.00	.03	−.05	−.04
American Telephone and Telegraph	−.04	−.10	.00	.03	.01	−.01	.01	.03	−.01	−.01
American Tobacco	.11	−.11	−.06	−.07	.00	−.04	−.01	.05	.04	−.04
Anaconda	.07	−.06	−.05	−.00	−.05	−.10	.01	.02	−.01	−.06
Bethlehem Steel	.01	−.07	.01	.02	−.02	.01	.04	.06	−.00	−.02
Chrysler	.01	−.07	−.02	−.01	−.00	.01	.02	.01	−.04	.02
du Pont	.01	−.03	.06	.03	−.00	−.05	.01	.01	−.03	.00
Eastman Kodak	.03	.01	−.03	.01	−.02	.01	−.01	−.01	.01	.00
General Electric	.01	−.04	−.02	.03	−.00	.00	−.01	−.01	−.00	.01
General Foods	.06	−.00	.05	.00	−.02	−.05	−.01	−.01	−.02	−.02
General Motors	−.00	−.06	.04	−.01	−.04	.01	.02	−.01	−.02	.01
Goodyear	−.12	.02	−.04	.04	−.00	−.00	.04	−.01	−.05	−.02
International Harvester	−.02	−.03	−.03	.04	−.05	−.02	−.00	.00	−.02	−.02
International Nickel	.10	−.03	−.02	.02	.03	.06	−.04	−.01	−.00	.03
International Paper	.05	−.01	−.06	.05	.05	−.00	−.03	−.02	−.02	−.02
Johns-Manville	.01	−.04	−.03	−.02	−.03	−.08	.04	.02	.04	.03
Owens-Illinois	−.02	−.08	−.05	.07	.00	−.04	.01	−.04	.07	.04
Procter and Gamble	.10	.01	−.01	.01	−.02	.02	.01	−.01	−.02	−.02
Sears Roebuck	.10	.03	.03	.03	−.01	−.05	−.01	−.01	−.07	−.01
Standard Oil	.01	−.12	.02	.01	−.05	−.02	−.02	−.03	.01	−.08
Standard Oil, California	.03	−.03	.05	−.03	−.05	−.03	−.01	.07	−.05	−.04
Swift Industries	−.00	−.02	−.01	−.01	.06	.01	−.04	.01	−.01	.00
Texaco	.09	−.05	−.02	−.02	−.02	−.01	.03	.03	−.01	.01
Union Carbide	.11	−.01	.04	.05	−.04	−.03	.00	−.01	−.05	−.04
United Aircraft	.01	−.03	−.02	−.05	−.07	−.05	.05	.04	.02	−.02
U.S. Steel Corp.	.04	−.07	.01	.01	−.01	−.02	.04	.04	−.02	−.04
Westinghouse	−.03	−.02	−.04	−.00	.00	−.04	−.02	.01	−.01	−.01
Woolworth	.03	−.02	.02	.01	.01	−.02	.00	.00	−.09	−.01
Averages	.03	−.04	−.01	.01	−.01	−.02	.00	.01	−.02	−.01

Source: E. F. Fama, 'The Behaviour of Stock Market Prices', *Journal of Business* (January 1965).

$$+ - + - + - + - + - + - + - + - + - + - \qquad (7.13)$$

you would probably strongly suspect that the tosses were not independent – there are too many runs (20). If, on the other hand you obtained the sequence

$$+ + + + + + + + + + - - - - - - - - - - - \qquad (7.14)$$

you would probably still not accept that the tosses were independent – this time there are too few runs (2).

The above principle has been applied by several economists, including, for example, Fama, to test the independence of stock price movements.[3] The results of such tests broadly confirm the correlation test results quoted earlier – namely the absence of any significant departure from randomness in any of the large number of stocks to which the test was applied.

Filter Tests

Before discussing the nature of filter tests for randomness in price movements, it will be convenient to briefly digress here in order to examine the type of information that the history of a share's price movements might convey to the investor – assuming of course that it conveyed any information at all.

Consider Figure 7.5(i), which depicts the behaviour of a share's price randomly fluctuating around its equilibrium value P_e. Thus P_e by definition is the value which the market professionals – the most fully informed investors – attach to that share, and any significant movement in the market price above or below P_e will present opportunities for capital gains to astute investors who can either go long or short according to whether the market price drifts below or above P_e.

However, small departures from P_e will be tolerated, principally because brokerage and information costs would outweigh any potential gains which such small movements might generate; but large departures from P_e will not be tolerated for the reason given above, and the points at which the professionals will intervene in the market are given by P_u and P_1 respectively.

The effect of the arrival of a new piece of (favourable) news at time t_0 will be to alter the underlying equilibrium price from P_e to, say, P'_e, as illustrated in Figure 7.5(ii), and the resulting band will also move upwards in a corresponding manner. If the market is not efficient, in the manner in which that term was defined at the beginning of this chapter, then the stock's price will not move instantaneously to its new equilibrium level P'_e but will rather begin a steady upward movement towards that point (in the manner of Figure 7.1).

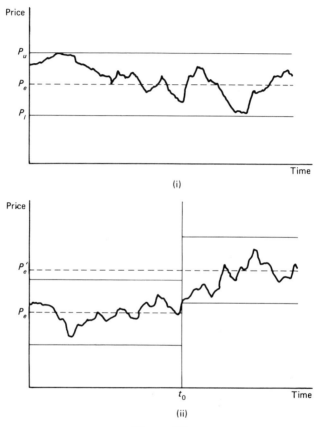

Figure 7.5

The investor, in interpreting the movements in the stock's price, will be attempting to discern whether the most recent changes are of the secondary type depicted in Figure 7.5(i), or whether they signal a fundamental change in the underlying equilibrium price – in other words, whether they are primary movements. If they are of the former type then he should ignore them – their information content is negligible. However, if they are of the latter type then (in this example) he should move in and purchase the stock with a view to generating capital gains as the upward movement towards the new higher equilibrium continues.

In what way might such an investor distinguish primary from secondary movements? P_e is of course unobservable as indeed are P_u and P_1. These are simply theoretical constructs. If, however, he knew the width of the band $P_u - P_1$, then any movement which took the stock's price outside the band would be clear evidence of the presence of a primary movement. This leads to consideration of the concept of a 'filter', which is a range of price variation within which a movement is regarded as secondary and outside of which it is regarded as primary. Thus a 10 per cent filter, for example, would provide the following decision rule for the investor: if the stock's price rises by more than 10 per cent above its previous low, buy it; if it declines by more than 10 per cent below its previous high, sell it.

Clearly, the size of the filter is a matter of choice and depends upon one's view as to the width of the band $P_u - P_1$. A large filter will result in fewer decisions to buy and sell, since large variations in the price of a stock occur less frequently than small ones. Thus a conservative investor who wished to ensure buying/selling only when a primary movement was taking place would tend to use a large filter. However, the penalty for such conservatism is that in many cases the primary move will be almost, if not totally, complete by the time he recognises it as such.

On the other hand, an investor who uses a small filter, say 1 per cent, would pay the penalty of making too many false moves – buying/selling when no primary movement was under way. He would be continually jumping the gun and consequently paying out an excessive amount in brokerage charges because of his frequent and needless buying and selling.

However, the investor who chooses the correct filter – that which corresponds to the width of the band $P_u - P_1$ – would correctly identify the primary movements and would consequently achieve a higher rate of return on his wealth than if he had followed a 'buy and hold' strategy. This latter strategy is implied by the random-walk hypothesis whenever the only information available to the investor is the history of the shares' prices. A 'buy and hold' strategy involves, as the term indicates, purchasing the security at the outset and holding it until the end, with no intermediate buying/selling as indicated by the use of a filter.

The relevance of the filter rule to the random-walk hypothesis is that the former will outperform a 'buy and hold' strategy *only on the assumption that the market is not efficient.* If the market is efficient, as the random-walk hypothesis asserts, then the filter will convey no useful information to the investor, irrespective of its size, since the movement to P'_e subsequent on the arrival of new information will take place instantaneously – leaving only secondary (random) price movements to follow from which no profit can be made.

In the light of the above discussion, a comparison between the rates of return achieved, under various filter rules and the rate of return achieved by a 'buy and hold' strategy would appear to be a valid test of the random-walk hypothesis. Several researchers have used the filter-test approach to investigate the random-walk phenomenon.[4]

The results of these experiments also conform to the general pattern described earlier. From the practical point of view there is no filter test which will achieve a higher rate of return than that achieved under the 'buy and hold' strategy. The Fama and Blume experiment,[5] for example, tested filters ranging from 0.5 per cent to 20.0 per cent. The average rate of return over a five-year period, using filters, was 2.7 per cent (before brokerage costs), compared with a 'buy and hold' figure of 9.9 per cent. The only filter that outperformed the 'buy and hold' strategy was the smallest (0.5 per cent), and that only marginally. However, when brokerage costs were taken into account, the performance of the filter rules deteriorated markedly, yielding an average annual rate of return of -19.1 per cent, compared with the 'buy and hold' figure of 9.9 per cent. This comparison illustrates the enormous cost in terms of brokerage fees of implementing the filter rule. However, even ignoring brokerage fees, the filter-rule approach to share purchases still produces substantially inferior rates of return to the 'buy and hold' strategy – thus lending yet further support to the random-walk hypothesis.

Technical, or Chart, Analysis

Technical, or chart, analysis is the term applied to the work of a particular school of stock-market analysts whose theories of stock price movements rely heavily on the use and interpretation of various types of charts or graphs. 'Chartists', as they are sometimes called, base their theories on a single fundamental belief, namely that in order to predict the future behaviour of a particular share price – or of the stock market as a whole – it is only necessary to examine the past pattern of price movements. This past pattern is seen as a consequence of, and thus as reflecting, the behaviour and belief of the thousands of individuals engaged in buying and selling securities. Consequently, chartists consider that it contains clues and pointers about the 'psychology', or mood, of the market at any particular time.

To refer to chart analysis as 'technical analysis' is not to imply that other theories of stock price behaviour are non-technical – in the sense of being non-scientific. It is rather meant to distinguish the work of the chartist from 'fundamental analysis', which is an attempt to predict stock price movements on the basis of future movements in the fundamental characteristics of the company which has issued the stock. (By the 'fundamental characteristics' of a company is meant such things as its capital structure, vulnerability to changes in the general economic climate, the state of its management–labour relations, and many other similar characteristics.)

Chartists, as opposed to fundamental analysts, believe that it is unnecessary to determine the fundamental source of the change in a share's price. They consider that the history of the share's price movements, as summarised in their own charts, contains all the information that is necessary in order to make predictions about the direction of future price changes.

Chartist analysts have never attained respectability among the majority of academic stock-market theorists – the latter maintaining that chartists have patently failed to substantiate their claim that technical analysis can predict the future direction of share price movements.

In order to appreciate the unruffled reaction of chartists to the above charge it is only necessary to bear in mind that they regard their work as an art rather than as a science, and consequently as not being amenable to objective validation or refutation. The same chart will be interpreted differently by different chartists, and thus when we attempt to check the validity of a chart's predictions, we 'end up testing the performance of the man rather than the method'.[6]

CHARTISTS' CHARTS

If technical analysis is to be regarded as an art, then the chart is the medium through which that art is expressed. Many different types of charts are used by chartists. However, the following description is not by any means an exhaustive account of the techniques used, but is rather a selection of some of the major ones.[7] It is intended to give the flavour, rather than the substance, of the work of the technical analyst.

The Line Chart

The line chart, of which Figure 7.6 is a schematic illustration, is the most familiar way in which the history of a share's price movements may be recorded. It is an ordinary time series, with the share's price on the vertical axis and time on the horizontal axis.

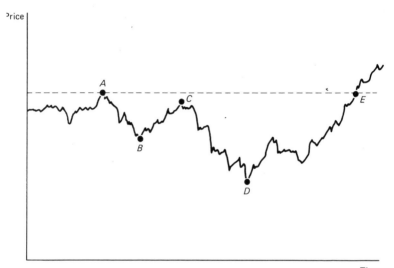

Figure 7.6

Line charts are used by technical analysts in the application of the *Dow theory*. According to this theory, trends in a stock's price movements may be classified as either 'primary' or 'secondary', and the objective of the chartist is to distinguish the underlying primary trend from those price movements which are merely of a secondary nature. Thus if the primary trend is a downward one, the chartist will predict further declines in the share's price irrespective of any recent (secondary) upward movements.

A chartist looking at Figure 7.6, for example, might make the following observations:

(i) At point *C* the stock has made an *abortive recovery*, in that it had been moving upwards from a low of B towards its historical high A, but the recovery (which peaked at C) stopped short before the historical high was reached. An abortive recovery is a bad omen, and is indicative of a downward primary trend.

(ii) The movement from C to D is particularly ominous in that the price penetrated the previous *reaction low* (namely B) – a reaction low being regarded by investors as a floor below which the stock's price should not fall. Other things being equal, any tendency for the price to fall below the reaction low should trigger a rash of buying orders from investors who would now regard the stock as being on offer at a bargain price. The fact that this has not happened in Figure 7.6 and that the reaction low has been penetrated would be regarded by the chartist as indicative of a new downward primary influence on the stock's price. The fact that the market has allowed the price to fall below its previous reaction low is very likely the consequence of some event which adversely affected the fortunes of the company. The chartist however is not concerned with the fundamental reason for the movement. By his own terms of reference, he acquires all the information he requires solely by examining the chart.

(iii) Last, the movement of the price beyond E constitutes the penetration of a previous reaction high and is a favourable indication that the primary price trend is an upward one.

The Bar Chart

The bar chart, depicted in Figure 7.7, instead of illustrating a single price for each time period (day, week, or whatever) as in the case of the line chart, shows by means of a vertical line the actual range of prices at which trading takes place during the period. The closing price is denoted by means of a small mark on the right-hand side of the bar.

Bar charts usually contain, on a separate scale at the foot of the chart, the volume of transactions which occurred during the period, as in Figure 7.7. The bar chart is more informative than the line chart, and consequently is preferred by the technical analyst in his search for underlying patterns. The volume of transactions figures at the foot of the bar chart give an indication of the strength of the market in the stock. Thus, for example, a rapid upward movement in a stock's price, in conjunction with a large amount of trading in that stock, is a much more optimistic market signal than if the same upward movement in the price took place in a thin market. It is customary in bar charts to include a box containing a history of the share's price ranges over the last, say, ten years together with data on recent earnings and dividends, as illustrated in Figure 7.7.

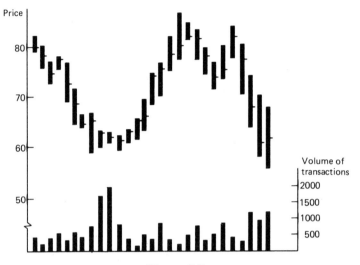

Figure 7.7

The Point and Figure Chart

Point and figure charting is a technique for recording all significant movements in a share's price. The decision as to what constitutes a significant movement is at the discretion of the chartist, and depends partly on the price of the share. Thus a movement of half a point in a share's price from $32\frac{1}{4}$p to $32\frac{3}{4}$p might appropriately be considered 'significant', whereas a half-point movement from $352\frac{1}{4}$p to $352\frac{3}{4}$p would obviously be less so.

Point and figure charts are simple to construct once the underlying principle behind them is grasped. A chart consists of a number of columns, each consisting entirely of either *x* or *o*, as in Figure 7.8. The number of *x*s in a column indicates the number of consecutive significant upward price movements that occur before a reversal, and the number of *o*s the number of consecutive significant downward price movements that occur before a reversal.

When a reversal occurs in a share's price movements – say it stops moving up and begins to move down – a new column is started on the chart, the old column being abandoned. Columns of *x*s are built from the bottom up; columns of *os* from the top down. As may be seen from Figure 7.8, there is no time scale on the chart, though it is conventional and useful to mark the passage of years on the horizontal axis as shown, and to substitute the number of the month for an *x* or an *o* as appropriate whenever the current change occurs in a different month than the previous one. An example will make all of this a little clearer.

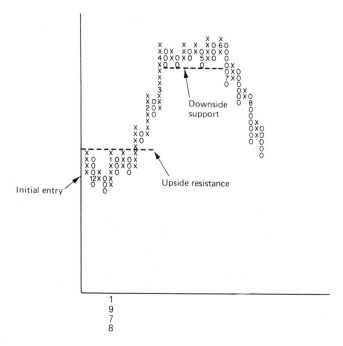

Figure 7.8 *Point and figure chart*

In order to illustrate the principles involved in the construction of a point and figure chart, let us construct a one-point chart for the stock with the price history described in Table 7.2. For a one-point chart we will make an entry whenever the stock's price changes by or through a whole number. If the price moves through more than one whole number in a given day, place the same number of *xs* or *os* on the chart as the number of units by which the price has changed. If the price does not move sufficiently during a given day's trading, do not make any entry in the chart for that day.

Referring to Table 7.2, we see that on 23 November the price

moved up by one and a half points from the previous day. Consequently we place one *x* – marked with an arrow – on the chart. On
24 November the price moved up by half a point to $77\frac{3}{4}$, so we make
no entry for that day. Note, however, that if the price had risen to 78
we would have made an entry even though the price would only have
moved by half a point during that day. The reason is that it would
have moved *through* the point 78 or, to put it another way, we already
have half a point yet to be credited as a result of the one and a half
point movement on 23 November.

Table 7.2

Date	Price		Date	Price
22 Nov	76		1 Dec	75
23 Nov	$77\frac{1}{2}$		2 Dec	$77\frac{1}{2}$
24 Nov	$77\frac{3}{4}$		3 Dec	$75\frac{1}{4}$
25 Nov	$79\frac{1}{4}$		4 Dec	74
26 Nov	$80\frac{1}{2}$		5 Dec	$74\frac{1}{2}$
29 Nov	80		6 Dec	$76\frac{1}{4}$
30 Nov	76		7 Dec	$77\frac{1}{2}$

On 25 November the price moves through 79, so we place two
further *x*s on the chart – since the last point recorded was 77. The
following day we record our fourth *x* for the move through 80, which
marks the end of the upward movement. On 30 November the price
moves down four points to 76, so we start a new column of *o*s with four
entries (starting from the top). Notice that the first entry in the
column of *o*s is one step below the top entry in the previous column of
*x*s. A little reflection will convince the reader that this adjustment is
necessary in order to ensure an *x* of a given height will represent the
same price no matter which column it appears in. For exactly the
same reason the first entry in a column of *x*s starts one step above the
last entry in the previous column of *o*s.

The primary objective in constructing point and figure charts is to
identify areas of *congestion* in a share's price, also known as *upside
resistance areas*, or *downside support areas*. These are extended bands of
price fluctuations within which price movements are of no particular
importance. However, any break-out from such areas of congestion
may be interpreted as indicating a new trend, or primary movement,
in the share's price, and such a break-out provides the buying/selling
signal for the chartist.

Conclusion

The issue as to whether security markets in general are efficient or not is still an open one. Nevertheless, the bulk of the available evidence lends support to the view that they are. The random-walk hypothesis has been subjected to numerous tests in many different markets and over different time periods and has invariably proved to be well supported by the available data. It is worth noting, however, that chartism, by its very nature, tends to produce self-fulfilling prophecies. To the extent that a large number of people believe that a share's price is about to move up and that the time is right to buy, their very act of purchasing the share will inevitably exert an upward pressure on its price, so validating their earlier predictions.

CHAPTER 8

Multi-period Portfolio Management

The theory of portfolio selection elaborated in the earlier chapters was developed implicitly within a *single-time-period* framework; that is to say, it was assumed that the investor consumed his wealth at the end of the single period over which he held the portfolio. In practice, however, the problem of managing an investment portfolio is an on-going commitment covering many time periods. Indeed, the typical institutional investors, such as the banks and insurance companies, may have an infinite horizon.

This consideration raises two new issues in the development of portfolio-selection theory. First, if the investor does intend to hold his portfolio for more than one time period, should he plan its composition for more than one period ahead, or should he simply take each day as it comes? Second, are the statistical characteristics (i.e. the means, variances and covariances) of the securities in the asset universe liable to change from one period to the next in such a way that a portfolio which was optimal at time it was chosen may become sub-optimal due to such changes?

This chapter is devoted to the development of a theoretical framework for multi-period portfolio-selection theory and, by implication, to the analysis of the two issues raised above.

Multi-period Portfolio-selection Framework

At first sight, the problem of whether to plan the composition of one's portfolio more than one period in advance might appear to be a trivial one. One might be tempted to argue heuristically that the best way to proceed in managing a multi-period portfolio is to select the optimal portfolio for the coming time period, at the end of which one merely recalculates the new optimal portfolio for the following time period, and makes whatever adjustments are necessary to one's current holdings of stocks to bring them into line with the new desired holdings.

Despite its possible intuitive appeal, however, the above procedure will not in general be optimal. For one thing, adjusting from an old to a new portfolio is not a costless activity, involving, as it does, the payment of brokerage charges, the cost of acquiring new information, and so on. Consequently, it will generally be desirable to anticipate the future composition of one's portfolio in order to keep such changes to a minimum.

A second weakness in the above approach arises when the investor's utility function is formulated in terms of rate of return (r) rather than terminal wealth (W_T). It will be recalled from page 20 that in the former case the investor's coefficient of risk aversion is a function of the level of initial wealth, so that such an investor's utility function will itself change in each time period as his initial wealth (at the beginning of that time period) varies due to the return on his assets during the previous time period. Consequently, even if there is no change in the statistical characteristics of the individual assets, his desired portfolio will be constantly changing through time as a result of his changing level of wealth.

However, perhaps the greatest weakness in the above approach is that it is *myopic*, or short-sighted. In general we do not find it optimal to plan our daily affairs in such a myopic fashion, so we should be surprised if the long-term management of a financial portfolio could be optimally carried out in this manner.

In developing a general framework for multi-period portfolio-selection theory, we will find it convenient to begin with a simple one-period model which can then be generalised to a two-period, and finally to the T-period, case.

THE ONE-PERIOD CASE

Consider first of all the following simple one-period portfolio-selection problem: an investor with initial wealth W_0 wishes to divide it between a safe asset (assumed here to be a riskless bond) and a risky asset (assumed here to be the market portfolio) so as to maximise the expected utility of terminal wealth (W_T) – *terminal* in this case meaning *at the end of the single holding period*.

Let the safe asset bear a rate of interest i, and let the market portfolio, labelled M, have an expected rate of return E_m and a variance

V_m. The investor's utility function is assumed to be quadratic in W_T and is

$$U(W_T) = W_T - \beta W_T^2. \tag{8.1}$$

His problem, then, is to choose an optimal amount of money, w, to be invested in the risky asset (i.e. the market portfolio), where w lies between zero and W_0, so as to maximise the expected utility of terminal wealth:

$$\max_{w} E[U(W_T)] \tag{8.2}$$
$$\text{subject to: } 0 \leqslant w \leqslant W_0$$

Letting the actual return on the risky asset be R, one can express terminal wealth as

$$W_T = W_0(1 + i) + w(R - i), \tag{8.3}$$

for any chosen value of w. Thus the investor's problem may be restated as

$$\max E[\{W_0(1 + i) + w(R - i)\} - \beta\{W_0(1 + i) + w(R - i)\}^2], \tag{8.4}$$

which, on multiplying out and collecting terms, can be rewritten as

$$\max E[C_0 + C_1 w + C_2 w^2], \tag{8.5}$$

where $C_0 = W_0(1 + i)(1 - \beta W_0(1 + i))$, $C_1 = (R - i)(1 - 2\beta W_0(1 + i))$, and $C_2 = -\beta(R - i)^2$. Since both C_0 and w are non-stochastic, expression (8.5) may be rewritten as

$$\max C_0 + E[C_1]w + E[C_2]w^2, \tag{8.6}$$

but

$$E[C_1] = (E_m - i)(1 - 2\beta W_0(1 + i)) = \tilde{C}_1, \tag{8.7}$$

and, recalling that $E[R^2] = E_m^2 + V_m$,

$$E[C_2] = \beta\{i(2E_m - i) - (E_m^2 + V_m)\} = \tilde{C}_2. \tag{8.8}$$

The investor's problem may now be rewritten as

$$\max_{w} C_0 + \tilde{C}_1 w + \tilde{C}_2 w^2. \tag{8.9}$$

This problem is solved by differentiating expression (8.9) with respect to w, setting the derivative equal to zero, and solving the resulting equation for w; thus

$$\tilde{C}_1 + 2\tilde{C}_2 w = 0. \tag{8.10}$$

Therefore

$$w_{\text{opt}} = \frac{\tilde{C}_1}{-2\tilde{C}_2} = \frac{(E_m - i)(1 - 2\beta(1 + i)W_0)}{2\beta\{(E_m^2 + V_m) - (i2E_m - i)\}}. \tag{8.11}$$

In the case where the riskless asset is cash (bearing a zero interest rate), setting $i = 0$ in the above yields

$$w_{\text{opt}} = \frac{E_m(1 - 2\beta W_0)}{2\beta(E_m^2 + V_m)}. \tag{8.12}$$

From an inspection of expressions (8.11) and (8.12), it is clear that the optimal amount, w_{opt}, which the investor should place in the risky asset depends upon his aversion to risk (β), his initial wealth (W_0), as well as the characteristics of the risky asset (E_m and V_m). The problem and solution are illustrated graphically in Figure 8.1.

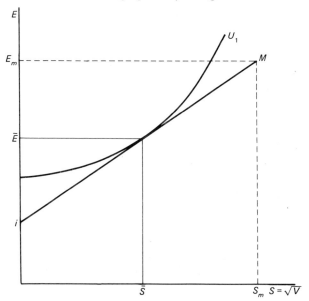

Figure 8.1

The line iM is the locus of attainable $[E, V]$ combinations depending upon the choice of w. The highest attainable level of utility is represented by the indifference curve U_1, and the point of tangency between U_1 and iM corresponds to the characteristics of the optimal portfolio, E and S.

It is worth noting that in equations (8.11) and (8.12) not only does the amount of money invested in the risky asset (w) depend upon initial wealth (W_o), but so also does the fraction of wealth w/W_o invested in the risky asset. Moreover, this fraction falls as initial wealth increases, thereby implying that the investor becomes more conservative as he gets richer. This characteristic is known as *increasing absolute risk-aversion*, and is a characteristic of all quadratic utility functions.

If we substitute the value of w_{opt} obtained in equation (8.11) into expression (8.9), we then have an expression for the maximum value of expected utility which the investor succeeds in attaining. This is the level of utility represented by the indifference curve U_1 in Figure 8.1, and is given by

$$\max E[U(W_T)] = k_1 + k_2\{W_o - (1+i)\beta W_o^2\}, \quad (8.13)$$

where k_1 and k_2 are constants (involving the parameters of the problem) which are of no direct interest to us and so, for simplicity, are not written out in full. While in the single-period case, equation (8.13) is of no great significance – given the ordinal nature of utility – we shall see that it plays an important role in the solution to the multi-period problem.

THE TWO-PERIOD CASE

The two-period portfolio-selection model is the simplest possible example of the class of multi-period models, but goes a long way towards illustrating the nature of the problems that arise in the multi-period context. The general structure of all such multi-period models is that the length of time over which the portfolio is to be held is split up into a number of *periods* (days, weeks, months, or whatever), and only at the beginning of such periods may changes be made in the composition of the portfolio, all such changes being binding until the beginning of the following period. We shall not consider here the case in which intermediate consumption is allowed to the investor.[1] The investor's objective is assumed to be the maximisation of the expected utility of his wealth at the end of the final time period.

Consider the following two-period problem in which the investor has an initial endowment of W_0. Let W_1 denote his wealth at the end of the first period, and W_2 his wealth at the end of the second period. His objective is then assumed to be

$$E[U(W_2)]. \tag{8.14}$$

As in the previous case, the asset universe consists of a riskless bond bearing a rate of interest i, and a single risky asset having an expected rate of return E_m and variance of return V_m. These characteristics are assumed to remain unchanged during the two periods for which the portfolio is held. Furthermore, the realised rates of return on the risky asset (R_t, $t = 1,2$) are assumed to be statistically independent, so that the covariance between them is zero. The realised rates of return on the two assets in the first period are thus i and R_1, and in the second period i and R_2.

Let w_1 be the amount invested in the risky asset in the first period, and w_2 be the amount invested in the risky asset in the second period. The investor's problem is then to maximise expression (8.14) by choosing the optimal values of w_1 and w_2. We assume here that his utility function is quadratic, as in the previous case.

We shall find it rewarding to tackle this problem by starting at the end, as it were, and working our way back to the beginning. This approach, which is commonly employed in the solution of multi-period problems, is described as 'backward recursive'. If the investor were already at the beginning of the second period, with wealth W_1, the remaining portfolio-selection problem would be a simple one-period one, namely to choose w_2 so as to maximise $E[U(W_2)]$. The solution to this problem has already been derived in equation (8.11), from which it is clear that the optimal value of w_2 is a function of initial wealth at the beginning of the period – in this case W_1.

In the present circumstances, equation (8.11) does not tell us the actual amount of money to be invested in the risky asset in the second time period – for the reason that at the outset of the problem the investor is not able to say with certainty what figure W_1 will be. What equation (8.11) does provide, however, is a *decision rule* which specifies for the investor the amount w_2 corresponding to any given value of W_1.

We already know, from equation (8.13), that once the optimal level of w_2 has been selected, the maximum level of expected utility which the investor can attain is given by

$$\max E[U(W_2)] = k_1 + k_2\{W_1 - (1 + i)\beta W_1^2\}. \tag{8.15}$$

Equation (8.15) is known as the investor's *indirect utility function*, in that it expresses the outcome of the problem in terms of the variable W_1. The next stage is to recall that W_1 is itself related to the first period decision variable, w_1, by the definition

$$W_1 = W_o(1 + i) + w_1(R_1 - i), \qquad (8.16)$$

and so by substituting for W_1 in equation (8.15) we can express the solution to the problem as a function of w_1. It follows, then, that the task facing the investor at the beginning of the first period is to choose w_1 so as to maximise his indirect utility function equation, (8.15). It can readily be shown that k_1 is a positive constant,[2] and so the maximisation of the whole function is achieved by maximising the expression inside the braces. This is essentially the same objective as that expressed in equation (8.15), with the slight modification that in this case β is replaced by $(1 + i)\beta$, and for w now read w_1. Not surprisingly, the solution to the present problem is directly analogous to the solution to expression (8.4) as given in expression (8.11), with the same modifications in notation:

$$(w_1)_{\text{opt}} = \frac{(E_m - 1)(1 - 2\beta(1 + i)^2 W_o)}{2\beta(1 + i)\{(E_m^2 + V_m) - i(2E_m - i)\}}. \qquad (8.17)$$

This completes the solution to the two-period problem, since the optimal value of w_1 can be calculated directly from equation (8.17); and at the end of the first period, when R_1 determines the actual value of W_1, the investor's decision rule (equation (8.11)) will yield a specific optimal value for w_2.

The above procedure is illustrated by the following numerical example.

Numerical Example

All the relevant information is presented in Table 8.1. The solution to the problem consists of the actual choice of w_1 and the decision rule for w_2. The optimal value of w_1 is readily calculated by inserting the appropriate values in formula (8.17), to give

$$w_1 = \text{\pounds}339,$$

and the decision rule for w_2 is obtained in an equally straightforward manner by inserting the appropriate values in formula (8.11) bearing in mind that for W_o in that formula we now read W_1, since W_1 is the relevant initial wealth in this case), to give

$$w_2 = \text{\pounds}686.9 - 0.297\,W_1. \qquad (8.18)$$

Table 8.1

Initial wealth (W_0)	£1000.00
Coefficient of risk-aversion (β)	0.0002
Interest rate on riskless bond (i)	0.08 (i.e. 8 per cent)
Expected rate of return on risky asset (E_m)	0.15 (i.e. 15 per cent)
Variance of rate of return on risky asset (V_m)	0.25

There are two points of interest to note about this solution. First, it is clear that the decision rule for w_2 is valid only for a certain range of values of W_1. Equation (8.17) is plotted in Figure 8.2, from which it can be seen that w_2 falls to zero when initial wealth W_1 reaches £2313. At this level of wealth the investor has become so conservative that he is no longer willing to invest any money in the risky asset. At the other end of the scale, it is clear that the investor can never invest more than his total wealth in the risky asset, and for low levels of wealth equation (8.18) requires him to do just that! In Figure 8.2 the dashed line plots the locus of points where $w_2 = W_1$ and it is only points below that line which are attainable. At all levels of wealth up to £530 the investor will put everything into the risky asset, but once that figure has been exceeded he begins to diversify.

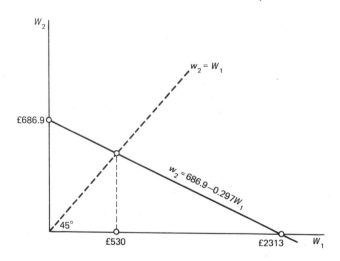

Figure 8.2

The second point of interest about the above solution is that it illustrates the fact that a myopic approach to the multi-period problem is sub-optimal. An investor solving the problem one period at a time, without reference to future periods, would simply apply formula (8.11) in each period, giving a figure of £390 for w_1 compared with the optimal figure of £339. Such a policy would result in the investor attaining a lower level of expected utility than if he had followed the optimal policy outlined above.

Statistical Appendix

This appendix reviews those elements of statistical theory which are most frequently used in the portfolio-selection literature. Readers who have taken an introductory course in statistics will probably already be familiar with most of the material contained here.

We begin by considering the concept of a *random variable* – that is, a variable the value of which is determined by some experiment of chance. If, for example, we set out on a journey, the length of time taken to arrive at our destination will be the result of a complicated experiment of chance – the level of traffic congestion, the probability of an accident or breakdown occurring, and so on. The random variable in question is the *length of time* taken and, if we split our measurement of time into discrete, say, five-minute intervals, we can denote the random variable by x_i, $i = 1, 2, 3, \ldots$ where $x_1 = 5$ minutes, $x_2 = 10$ minutes, and so on.

Attached to each x_i there is a *probability* that the journey will take that time. If it were possible to repeat the journey an infinite number of times we should be able to construct the *probability density function* (p.d.f.) of the random variable x. This is a function which assigns to each value of x_i the corresponding probability of it occurring. Such a p.d.f. is illustrated in Figure A.1, where the height of each column is a measure of the probability of the corresponding value of x occurring. Clearly, since the journey must take some finite time (assuming that we don't die on the way), the sum of these probabilities must add to unity.

Two questions that one might ask of the p.d.f. are (i) what is the average length of time for the journey? and (ii) can we expect to be usually quite close to the average time, or does the length of time taken vary a lot from day to day? These two questions may be answered by calculating the first and second *moments* of the p.d.f. respectively. The

134 Theory of Portfolio Selection

first moment is called the *mean* or *expectation* of the random variable and is denoted here by $E[x]$. It is calculated by adding up each value of x_i multiplied by its corresponding probability, which is denoted by p_i, thus

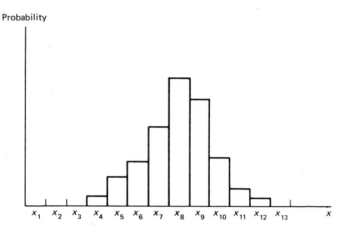

Probability

$$x_1 \quad x_2 \quad x_3 \quad x_4 \quad x_5 \quad x_6 \quad x_7 \quad x_8 \quad x_9 \quad x_{10} \quad x_{11} \quad x_{12} \quad x_{13} \qquad x$$

Figure A.1

$$E[x] = x_1 p_1 + x_2 p_2 + \ldots + x_k p_k \qquad (A.1)$$

where k is the number of possible outcomes. Using the summation operator Σ (defined on page 29) we can write equation (A.1) more compactly as

$$E[x] = \sum_{i=1}^{k} x_i p_i. \qquad (A.2)$$

Thus the first moment corresponds to the everyday notion of the 'average'. E is known as the *expectation operator* and has the following properties. Let a and b be constants and x and y be random variables, then

$$E[a + bx] = a + bE[x]. \qquad (A.3)$$

and

$$E[ax + by] = aE[x] + bE[y]. \qquad (A.4)$$

Equation (A.4) may be interpreted as saying that the expectation of a weighted sum of two or more random variables is simply the same weighted sum of their individual expectations.

The second moment of the distribution is known as the *variance* and is a measure of the extent to which the p.d.f. is concentrated close to its mean. (See Figure A.2.) Denoting the variance of the distribution as $V[x]$, it is calculated as follows:

$$V[x] = \sum_{i=1}^{k} (x_i - E[x])^2 p_i. \qquad (A.5)$$

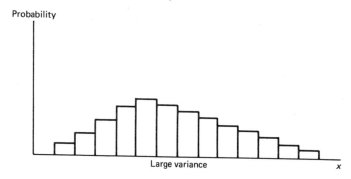

Large variance

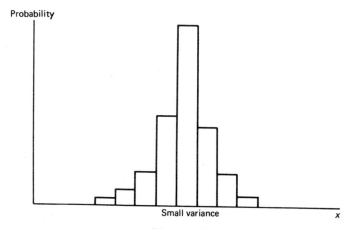

Small variance

Figure A.2

It is thus the sum of squared deviations of the individual xs from their mean, each weighted by the corresponding probability. It is the mean of the squared deviations and is clearly a measure of dispersion. Why not take the mean of the deviations (without squaring them) as a more straightforward measure of dispersion? The reason is that the resulting expression would always turn out to be zero. (Try proving this as an exercise.)

An alternative measure of dispersion is to take the mean of the deviations from the mean but ignore negative signs. This is known as the mean of the absolute deviations (M.A.D.) and is written as

$$\sum_{i=1}^{k} |x_i - E[x]| p_i \qquad (A.6)$$

where the two vertical bars mean that if the expression between them is a negative number the negative sign is ignored. As a measure of dispersion M.A.D. overcomes the problem described in the previous paragraph, but it is not popular as it is difficult to handle mathematically.

The square root of the variance is known as the *standard deviation* and is often used as a measure of dispersion instead of the variance. Clearly there is a one-to-one relationship between the variance and the standard deviation. Lastly the variance of a constant is zero since, by definition, a constant never varies from its mean value.

Let us turn next to consider the relationship between two random variables x and y. Let x have a mean $E[x]$ and variance $V[x]$, and let y have a mean $E[y]$ and variance $V[y]$. It may be useful to know if on those occasions on which x is above its mean value y is also above its mean, or alternatively whether y tends to be below its mean on such occasions. In order to answer this question we need to compute a *cross-moment*, the *covariance* between x and y. This is defined as

$$\text{cov}[x,y] = \sum_{i=1}^{k} (x_i - Ex)(y_i - Ey) p_i q_i \qquad (A.7)$$

where q_i is the probability attached to y_i. If both x and y tend to move together the covariance will be a positive number; if they tend to move in offsetting ways it will be a negative number; and if they move completely independently of one another it will be zero. However, the covariance is not a particularly useful measure of the relationship between two variables since its value depends upon the units of measurement of both x and y. Lastly note that the covariance between a variable and a constant is zero. (Why?)

A more useful measure of dispersion, and one which is invariant with respect to the units of measurement, is the *correlation coefficient* between x and y, and is defined as

$$\rho = \frac{\text{cov}(x,y)}{\sqrt{V[x].V[y]}} \tag{A.8}$$

The correlation coefficient is bounded below by the value -1.0, which corresponds to perfect negative correlation, and above by the value $+1.0$, which corresponds to perfect positive correlation.

Consider next the random variable z, which is a weighted combination of the random variables x and y, with weights w_1 and w_2 respectively:

$$z = w_1 x + w_2 y. \tag{A.9}$$

we already know from (A.4) that

$$E[z] = w_i E[x] + w_2 E[y] \tag{A.10}$$

but what of the variance of z? If we know the covariance between x and y we can express the variance of z as

$$V[z] = w_1^2 V[x] + w_2^2 V[y] + 2w_1 w_2 \text{cov}(x,y) \tag{A.11}$$

So far we have been discussing combinations of two variables. Let us generalise now to consider weighted combinations of any number of variables – say, n in number. A minor change in notation will facilitate matters here. Let the variables be known as $x_1, x_2, \ldots, x_n$ with means $E[x_1], E[x_2], \ldots, E[x_n]$ and let the covariance between x_i and x_j be called $\text{cov}(x_i, x_j)$. Consider a new random variable called p, which is a weighted combination of the xs with weights $w_1, w_2, \ldots, w_n$. How can we define the mean and variance of p? By a straightforward generalisation of (A.4) and (A.11) we get

$$E[p] = \sum_{i=1}^{n} w_i E[x_i] \tag{A.12}$$

and

$$V[p] = \sum_{i=1}^{u} \sum_{j=1}^{n} w_i w_j \text{cov}(x_i, x_j). \tag{A.13}$$

It should be clear from expression (A.7) that $\text{cov}(x_i, x_i)$ is simply $V(x_i)$.

Substituting x_1 and x_2 for x and y in expression (A.11) will convince that (A.13) is indeed the generalisation of (A.11).

Notes and References

Chapter 1

1. For an example of the application of the principles of portfolio-selection theory to the problem of the simultaneous selection of assets and liabilities, see M. Parkin, 'Discount House Portfolio and Debt Selection', *Review of Economic Studies* (1970) pp. 469–97.

2. The principles of financial analysis fall outside the scope of this book, and the interested reader is referred to the classic work of B. Graham, D. L. Dodd and S. Cottle, *Security Analysis* (New York: McGraw-Hill, 1962).

Chapter 2

1. See J. Hicks, *Value and Capital* (Oxford University Press, 1939).

2. See J. von Neumann and O. Morgenstern, *The Theory of Games and Economic Behaviour*, 2nd edn (Princeton University Press, 1947).

3. The proof of the expected utility theorem is not given here, but the interested reader is referred to R. D. Luce and H. Raiffa, *Games and Decisions* (New York: Wiley, 1967) pp. 19ff.

4. A proof of this property may be found in *ibid.* p. 30.

Chapter 4

1. For a full discussion of the relationship between risk and uncertainty, the reader is referred to the seminal contribution of F. Knight, *Risk, Uncertainty and Profit* (Boston, 1921).

2. H. M. Markowitz, *Portfolio Selection: Efficient Diversification of Investments* (New York: Wiley, 1959).

3. See E. F. Fama, 'The Behaviour of Stock Market Prices', *Journal of Business* (January 1965) pp. 34–105.

Chapter 5

1. The reader who is unfamiliar with the concepts of vectors and matrices will lose little, if any, of the content of what follows. However, since linear algebra is widely used in the literature, anyone wishing to pursue the subject seriously should consult a good text on the subject, for example, G. Hadley, *Linear Algebra* (Reading, Mass.: Addison-Wesley, 1961).

Chapter 6

1. W. F. Sharpe, 'A Simplified Model for Portfolio Analysis', *Management Science* (January 1963) pp. 277–93.

2. J. Lintner, 'The Valuation of Risk Assets and the Selection of Risky Investment in Stock Portfolios and Capital Budgets', *Review of Economics and Statistics* (February 1965) pp. 13–37.

3. J. L. Evans and S. H. Archer, 'Diversification and the Reduction of Dispersion: An Empirical Analysis', *Journal of Finance* (December 1968) pp. 761–9.

4. The technique involved is known as 'varimax rotation', and as a detailed discussion of it is beyond the scope of this book the interested reader is referred to D. Farrar. *The Investment Decision under Uncertainty* (Englewood Cliffs, N.J.: Prentice-Hall, 1962).

Chapter 7

1. E. F. Fama, 'The Behaviour of Stock Market Prices', *Journal of Business* (January 1965) pp. 34–105.

2. See, for example, M. G. Kendall, 'The Analysis of Economic Time-Series', *Journal of the Royal Statistical Society*, vol. 96, pt 1 (1953); A. B. Moore, 'Some Characteristics of Changes in Common Stock Prices', Doctoral Thesis, University of Chicago (1960) – excerpts reprinted in P. H. Cootner, *The Random Character of Stock Prices* (Cambridge: M.I.T. Press, 1964); T. M. Ryan, 'Security Prices as Markov Processes', *Journal of Financial and Quantitative Analysis* (January 1973) pp. 17–36.

3. Fama, 'The Behaviour of Stock Market Prices', op. cit.

4. See S. S. Alexander, 'Price Movements in Speculative Markets: Trends or Random Walks', *Industrial Management Review*, 2 (1961) pp. 7–26 – reprinted in P. H. Cootner, *The Random Character of Stock Prices* (Cambridge: M.I.T. Press, 1964); E. F. Fama and M. E.

Blume, 'Filter Rules and Stock Market Trading', *Journal of Business* (January 1966) pp. 226–41; J. C. van Horne and G. G. C. Parker, 'The Random Walk Theory: An Empirical Test', *Financial Analysts Journal* (November–December 1967) pp. 87–92.

5. Fama and Blume, 'Filter Rules and Stock Market Trading', op. cit.

6. J. B. Cohen and E. D. Zinbarg, *Investment Analysis and Portfolio Management* (Homewood, Ill.: Irwin, 1967) p. 521.

7. The interested reader is referred to *ibid.* ch. 14 and to the bibliography at the end of that chapter.

Chapter 8

1. The interested reader is referred to P. A. Samuelson, 'Lifetime Portfolio Selection by Dynamic Stochastic Programming', *Review of Economics and Statistics* (August 1969) pp. 23–34.

2. To verify that k_1 is positive, see J. Mossin, 'Optimal Multi-period Portfolio Policies', *Journal of Business* (April 1968) pp. 215–29.

Further Reading

K. J. Arrow, 'Alternative Approaches to the Theory of Choice in Risk Taking Situations', *Econometrica* (October 1951) pp. 404–37.

A. H. Y. Chen, F. C. Jen and S. Zionts, 'The Optimal Portfolio Revision Policy', *Journal of Business* (January 1971) pp. 51–61.

J. B. Cohen and E. D. Zinbarg, *Investment Analysis and Portfolio Management* (Homewood, Ill.: Irwin, 1967).

K. J. Cohen and J. A. Pogue, 'An Empirical Evaluation of Alternative Portfolio Selection Models', *Journal of Business* (April 1967) pp. 166–93.

P. H. Cootner, *The Random Character of Stock Prices* (Cambridge: M.I.T. Press, 1964).

E. J. Elton and M. J. Gruber, 'On the Optimality of Some Multi-period Portfolio Selection Criteria', *Journal of Business* (April 1974) pp. 231–43.

J. L. Evans and S. H. Archer, 'Diversification and the Reduction of Dispersion: An Empirical Analysis', *Journal of Finance* (December 1968) pp. 761–9.

E. F. Fama, 'The Behaviour of Stock Market Prices', *Journal of Business* (January 1965) pp. 34–105.

E. F. Fama, 'Efficient Capital Markets: A Review of Theory and Empirical Work', *Journal of Finance* (May 1970) pp. 383–417.

E. F. Fama, and M. E. Blume, 'Filter Rules and Stock Market Trading', *Journal of Business* (January 1966) pp. 226–41.

D. Farrar, *The Investment Decision Under Uncertainty* (Englewood Cliffs, N.J.: Prentice-Hall, 1962).

B. Graham, D. L. Dodd and S. Cottle, *Security Analysis* (New York: McGraw-Hill, 1962).

G. Hadley, *Linear Algebra* (Reading, Mass.: Addison-Wesley, 1961).

J. R. Hicks, *Value and Capital* (Oxford University Press, 1939).

M. G. Kendall, 'The Analysis of Economic Time-Series', *Journal of the Royal Statistical Society*, vol. 96, pt 1 (1953).

B. F. King, 'Market and Industry Factors in Stock Price Behaviour', *Journal of Business* (January 1966) pp. 139–90.

J. Lintner, 'The Valuation of Risk Assets and the Selection of Risky Investment in Stock Portfolios and Capital Budgets', *Review of Economics and Statistics* (February 1965) pp. 13–37.

R. D. Luce and H. Raiffa, *Games and Decisions* (New York: Wiley, 1967).

H. M. Markowitz, 'Portfolio Selection', *Journal of Finance* (March 1952).

H. M. Markowitz, *Portfolio Selection: Efficient Diversification of Investments* (New York: Wiley, 1959).

A. B. Moore, 'Some Characteristics of Changes in Common Stock Prices, Doctoral Thesis, University of Chicago (1960); excerpts reprinted in Cootner, *The Random Character of Stock Prices*.

J. Mossin, 'Optimal Multiperiod Portfolio Policies', *Journal of Business* (April 1968) pp. 215–29.

T. M. Ryan, 'Security Prices as Markov Processes', *Journal of Financial and Quantitative Analysis* (January 1973) pp. 17–36.

P. A. Samuelson, 'Lifetime Portfolio Selection by Dynamic Stochastic Programming', *Review of Economics and Statistics* (August 1969) pp. 23–34.

W. F. Sharpe, 'A Simplified Model for Portfolio Analysis', *Management Science* (January 1963) pp. 277–93.

K. V. Smith, 'Alternative Procedures for Revising Investment Portfolios', *Journal of Financial and Quantitative Analysis* (December 1968) pp. 371–403.

J. von Neumann and O. Morgenstern, *The Theory of Games and Economic Behaviour*, 2nd edn (Princeton University Press, 1947).

Index